HONORABLE CAT

BOOKS BY PAUL GALLICO

NOVELS

The Snow Goose
The Lonely
Jennie
Trial by Terror
The Small Miracle
Snowflake
The Foolish Immortals
Love of Seven Dolls
Mrs. 'Arris Goes to Paris
Ludmila
Thomasina
Flowers for Mrs. Harris
Mrs. Harris Goes to New York
Too Many Ghosts
Scruffy
Coronation
Love, Let Me Not Hunger
Three Stories
The Hand of Mary Constable
Mrs. 'Arris Goes to Parliament
The Man Who Was Magic
The Poseidon Adventure
Matilda
The Zoo Gang

GENERAL

The Steadfast Man: A Life of St. Patrick
The Hurricane Story
Confessions of a Storyteller
The Silent Miaow
The Story of Silent Night
Honorable Cat

FOR CHILDREN

The Day the Guinea-Pig Talked
The Day Jean-Pierre was Pignapped
The Day Jean-Pierre Went Round the World
Manxmouse
The Day Jean-Pierre Joined the Circus

HONORABLE CAT

BY
PAUL GALLICO

Photographs by Osamu Nishikawa

ADDITIONAL PHOTOGRAPHS BY VIRGINIA GALLICO

CROWN PUBLISHERS, INC.
New York

Cats of the world arise
This book is dedicated to you all
And your obvious superiority to mankind.
Arise! Unite! Take over!

P.G.

Published by Crown Publishers, Inc.,
201 East 50th Street, New York, New York 10022.
Member of the Crown Publishing Group.
Crown is a trademark of Crown Publishers, Inc.

Printed in Hong Kong

Library of Congress Cataloging-in-Publication Data

Gallico, Paul, 1897–
  Honorable cat.

  1. Cats—Literary collections. I. Nishikawa, Osamu,
1940-   . II. Gallico, Virginia. III. Title.
[PS3513.A413H6   1982]   811'.52   82-9193
                                              AACR2

ISBN 0-517-54887-9 (pbk.)
12   11   10   9   8   7

CONTENTS

NURSERY RHYMES FOR KITTENS

HONORABLE CAT

My Lives with Cats and What They Have Taught Me

IN justification of the above title it seems to me that first I ought to present my credentials. As a city boy born into turn-of-the-century New York, living through youth, adolescence, and later young manhood always in an apartment, I was never able to have an animal or pet of any kind. I craved both dog and cat but, as I remember, the cat was the more passionate longing. Circumstances permitted neither.

A city boy I remained until my thirty-ninth year, when I pulled up stakes and settled into a timbered house on the Devon Coast of England. There, temporarily freed of all encumbrances except ambition, my long suppressed desire burst from confinement in a veritable fireworks of cats, and in my cottage by the sea I gave houseroom to twenty-seven of the species and one Great Dane.

The Great Dane? Let us not lose sight of the fact that I had yearned also for a dog and, when freedom was achieved, indulged here as well. The Dane, in size and heft, added up to about twenty of the cats. He also appointed himself their guardian.

Twenty-seven cats at one time hints at monomania but in my case it was simpler. If you like cats and have some, you get kittens; and if you like kittens and enjoy having them about, they grow up and you get more cats.

Well then, perhaps it was batty but all the pent-up childhood longings were satisfied wholesale, so to speak. Indoors or out, during this period which lasted some three years, cats or kittens were never out of eyeshot; they played in the pigeonholes of my desk, interfered with my typing, hung from the curtains, or basked in the sun outside on the seawall. And out of them and myself and this first frustrated and then requited love came a book called *The Abandoned (Jennie)*.

Instinctively fleeing the urban terrors to come, I then lived on a farm in New Jersey, a hacienda in Mexico, in a chalet on a Liechtenstein mountaintop, a villa on Lake Como, and a beach house in Malibu in pursuit of the literary career, and everywhere there were cats.

I have consorted with practically all kinds, of every color and description; short-haired, long-haired, alley cat, show cat, Siamese, Abyssinian, tabby, tiger, black, white, orange, and every combination you can imagine; good cat, bad cat, sweet cat, sour cat, dull ones, bright ones, pompous and stuffy cats, and gay ones with an enchanting sense of humor. For cats vary, as do people, in their characters and characteristics and only when you deal with them over the years *en gros* do you know this. And yet withal, the essential mystery of their natures I have never been able to solve.

And now to what I may have learned.

Ailurophiles and Ailurophobes

ONE could, I suppose, arbitrarily divide the peoples of the world into two classifications, the ailurophiles and the ailurophobes, from the Greek, the philes being lovers of cats, the phobes those who hate or fear them.

There is a whole library of research on the phobia of those who cannot bear the cat and these fall into groups themselves: people who cannot endure them for psychological reasons having to do with their own natures; those who are subject to atavistic tremors in the face of this animal; and those who are definitely physically affected by their presence and react with disgust to the point of nausea or break out into allergic rashes.

But I have never seen a single line to explain why it is puss loves them one and all and if there is a phobe in the room will make a beeline for the party, purr, roll over, flatter, cajole, and jump up onto the victim's lap murmuring endearments.

Toward us philes who have the warmest affection for kitty on various levels and for many diverse reasons ranging from amused delight to love, the cat is able to show the utmost indifference. To an outpouring of fondness on our part, demonstrated by stroking it, scratching it, hugging it to us and crooning over it, cat will yawn and, as soon as our smothering hold upon it is released, get up, jump down, and go. This is understandable. Amorousness can be cloying and disagreeable, particularly if practiced at the wrong moment.

But as I say, never mind us philes. I have always thought I understood my cat's attitude toward my overreacting to it and respected it.

But what about the poor phobes? It would be simple to say that, feeling rejected, the animal is determined to win over such a one just to show him that it can be done. But that isn't cat. That is more a dog's characteristic. Cat simply doesn't care.

And besides, it is impossible. It isn't going to work ever. The phobe
is not to be reformed by such flattery. The presence of a cat fills him with
whatever you care to ascribe to that Greek root—fear, dread, horror, bad
memories, not to mention the physical problems already referred to, and
nothing is going to cure them.

Felis domestica most certainly would have found this out in its three-
or four-thousand-year association with human beings.

Well then, to return to our mystery, what is it? A gag, a perverted
sense of humor? Or, even, pity and compassion for someone who through
an illness is missing something out of life? I wouldn't put anything past
a cat.

Or if it were a kind of vengeance, a deliberate decision to increase
the discomfort of the sufferer, it would not surprise me. If the cat on the
one hand was deified and pampered, it has also been greatly sinned against,
and the history of its treatment down through the ages at the hands of
humans, as we know, shows the balance to be all against us. Is there some
ratiocination in whatever may be the mental processes of kitty that works
out to, "Hullo, I scent a prospect who, for one reason or another, cannot
bear me. Whoopee! Here's where I really spoil his day and chalk up one
for our side."

Or is it the powerful attraction of unlikes, the two opposite poles of
the magnets that leap to be joined together; the love-hate dependency
which is perhaps the basis of most relationships, human or animal? Is love
only truly to be distinguished by suffering and torment, and are the cats
and their phobes the only true lovers, and we philes but a pale reflection?

I have another suggestion: Is it the syndrome of the lady who is
convinced that she is the only one who can reform the hardened or habitual
drunk or wean the unhappy homosexual away from his affliction, even
though, with but the scantiest of exceptions, it has never been done?

And yet they will go on trying to do it. Is this cat's attempted seduc-
tion then, this irresistible challenge to accomplish the impossible, based
on arrogance or the mathematics of chance that it will be the one to achieve
the never-before-accomplished?

Well, this is certainly a human trait and I suppose we owe progress
to it. And since in one way or another, all human traits are derived from
our ancestors in the animal kingdom, it might not be too farfetched to
suggest that puss feels the same stirring of the pioneer spirit.

Thus we might look into the mind of a cat who has had the good
fortune to come home, walk into the living room, and find there an uptight
old gentleman who looks upon it with horror and loathing. There is the
challenge not to be declined and, already in its mind, puss is imagining
and savoring the future conversation of a couple of friends or neighbors
conferring on the back fence one night, the dialogue going something like
this:

"You heard what happened to old Tom?"

"No, nothing bad I hope."

"On the contrary, a miracle; an absolute miracle."

"Do tell."

"Well, as I got it, the other day he came home to find that his people had company, and knew immediately that the old codger seated in the drawing room was a phobe from way back. The lot. Hated everything about us. In fact would have got up out of the chair and left the room if Tom hadn't beat him to it and made his lap first. Tom said later he couldn't say why, he just knew that he had to have a go at reclaiming him. Sort of a sign from heaven kind of thing. Maybe you'd call it a revelation. Anyway, he gets up onto his lap before the old boy can move, then puts one paw on his cheek, rubs up against his ear, and purrs."

"Oh, my God, and then what?"

"You wouldn't believe this, but the next minute, the phobe is scratching Tom's head and saying, 'Why, you like me, don't you, kitty? Well, well, well.' But that isn't all. Tom heard that the old fellow had made a trip to the cats' home and actually adopted one of us."

"Go on! I'll be darned. You mean a clean breakthrough?"

"Looks like it. The affair, of course, is being investigated but if it stands up, old Tom is certain to be the first cat to be deified since Bubastis."

The above, you will recognize, is apocryphal but then so would you have considered the first thoughts of the man muttering to himself, "If I could solve the relationship of fuel consumption to weight, we could reach the moon." One has to try, doesn't one?

Have I exhausted the speculations? What else remains? Well, I suppose if we could but communicate in a mutually understandable language, an intimate chat of a few minutes might serve to clear up the whole enigma. But would it? On the record, whole races of people talk to one another from morning to night in a mutually understandable language and actually haven't the faintest idea what they are really saying to one another.

I leave you to get on with the problem if you are interested. Personally, I would dearly like to know.

Cats versus the Competition

THE cat competes for the hearts and minds of people, not to mention the freeloading privileges, with the dog, the monkey, the horse, the rabbit, and a variety of small rodents and birds kept in their pockets by little boys. We'll leave out birds as being too stupid even to be handicapped in the race. Incidentally, I am given to understand by those who know that the horse also rates high in the stupidity stakes. Furthermore, although one can love one's horse or donkey, one doesn't ordinarily let it inside the house. This would seem to limit the competition to those animals admitted, by normal people, into the living room.

These three, then, the dog, the cat, and the ape have learned to live with humans and adapt themselves to our own irrational behavior. And of the trio, I would give the cat the highest marks for intelligence and self-sufficiency, for the simple reason that whereas the first two species can be conditioned, the cat cannot except with the utmost difficulty. It is almost impossible to train it or teach it to do what we call "tricks." In fact, it is almost equally difficult to get it to do anything it doesn't want to do. This bespeaks to me a far higher level than has been achieved by man who much more easily than his feline friends can be conditioned, terrorized, or bribed into doing something his good sense tells him he had better not, including coming out from behind cover and walking into machine-gun fire. When a cat becomes aware of trouble ahead it goes the other way. Fast!

The behavior of the cat, with or without man, has always been the most sagacious. There's no need to look any further for proof than its survival and its success in establishing itself in the hearts and minds of people, without giving much away or relinquishing its independence.

While dogs touch me emotionally and I cannot resist their appeal they strike me, by and large, as being witless, hysterical, and mindless creatures except when one hears of a specimen who has had the sense to yap upon smelling or noting the house is on fire, or the courage to bite the burglar in the trousers, or the intelligence to fish a child out of the water. The manner in which the dog can be conditioned has brought the name of Pavlov into the language. They can actually be trained to point out where a square meal in the shape of a succulent bird is hiding in a bush or some gorse, instead of keeping the secret of their discovery to themselves. And after his equally dim master has caused the bird to fly up before shooting it, instead of sensibly potting it on the ground and thus making certain it gets into his oven, the dog then actually cooperates in an act of even more inexplicable stupidity: he sniffs out what ought to be a private and delectable meal for himself, takes it in his mouth, and fetches it back to the hunter. You wouldn't find any cat consenting to such lunatic behavior. This same cat will, however, often voluntarily donate a mouse to its family as an act either of love or gratitude. It is a most wondrous gift and, in my opinion, completely thought out beforehand.

This, and again it is one observer's opinion, leaves the monkey and the cat to fight it out in the intelligence stakes, and here it is the former who starts out with the tremendous advantage of looking like most of us, or vice versa.

The monkey, with his near-human face, his sad, near-human eyes and his near-human hands, is a constant reminder to us of our common ancestry and of the fact that these sometimes savage, more often pathetic, creatures perpetrated some fatal genetic error and were left behind. They say that it was their failure to develop further the use of the thumb that denied them a share in the invention of the flamethrower, poison gas, and the atom bomb, and that this skeletal deficiency interfered with the growth of their brains.

The apes sent on moon rides by the early experimental space explorers could be taught or conditioned to press a lever and feed themselves from whatever came out of the penny-in-the-slot machine, but a cat can learn all by itself how to open a door with a handle if it wants out. Perhaps this is not wholly fair, for the ape, given a problem such as a bit of food out of reach, can work it out by himself also by inventing an extension of his arm in the shape of a stick or a branch and can solve even more complicated puzzles. On the other hand, the ape has far better physical equipment for such solutions in the shape of its body and, above all, its hand, a kind of junior one. The cat is equipped to grasp nothing except by the use of its two forefeet pressed together, and yet the cat in the house manages its life and business very well.

The circus chimpanzee can be taught to eat at a table with a napkin around his neck, smoke a cigar, pound a drum or thump the keys of a piano, ride a bicycle or pretend to read a newspaper, but every so often during this performance I catch him throwing up a look of pleading or misery at his trainer, or most assuredly it is a look of uncertainty of some kind, almost as though at the very moment he is performing these human antics, he is being less human than ever he might become.

You wouldn't find any self-respecting cat involved in such indignities and humiliating shenanigans. Certain superior house cats will allow themselves to be dressed in dolls' clothes and mobcaps and set down to a miniature table for tea by their child companions, but this is purely a voluntary affair on their part, and devotion to the young.

I am willing to wager that in all the years as child and adult that you have been attending circuses you in all probability have never seen an act featuring trained cats. Big cats, yes; little cats, no.

It makes one wonder at what time in their development, when small cat parted from large cat via the process of natural selection and the demands of environment, that it acquired its good sense. Lions, tigers, leopards, panthers, and cheetahs can be conned into making fools of themselves and momentarily suppressing their natural desires to make mincemeat of their trainers. In addition to sitting up, rolling over, and forming pyramids, the big jungle *Felidae* can be taught to ignore that which they fear the most in their natural state, namely fire, and jump through flaming hoops. If you suggested such a thing to your house cat, it would, in my opinion, reach for the telephone and ask for the loony chariot to be sent over for you.

Dogs will play football, walk a tightrope, and do backflips; bears will roller-skate or ride seesaws, and seals render "My Country 'Tis of Thee" on a bank of tooters, but your pet cat won't even come when you call it if it doesn't feel like it or doesn't think there might be something in it for itself.

I won't say arbitrarily that the domestic cat cannot be trained. Anything can be done and there are cat trainers, men of infinite patience, but it isn't something on which you would want to count.

I'm thinking in particular of being on the set one time in England

when the late Walt Disney was engaged in shooting *Thomasina,* one of
my novels.

Thomasina, the cat of the story, was played by a ginger cat "trained"
by a trainer, with another for a stand-in and understudy. At one point in
the film Thomasina was required to do nothing more complicated than
walk across a ridgepole from one point to another, a feat which any feline
can accomplish with its eyes shut. The "take" had offered no problem
in rehearsal. We then lost two days shooting because Thomasina, for
whatever reasons she saw fit to entertain, decided she didn't want to
cross that ridgepole. Nothing could persuade her to do so. Voice command,
whistles, food, threats, and even a seductive gentleman cat positioned
at the far end. Not even, mind you, the presence and thunder of the great
God Walt himself. I was proud of that cat.

Dogs are dirty, monkeys are dirty (well, and I am afraid, too, that
people are dirty unless taught), but the cat, by instinct and heredity, is
scrupulously clean and even the most dejected and filthy alley bum will
be seen having a go every so often at washing himself, although with
the condition of our city streets it is bound to be a losing game.

Of the three, dog, ape, and cat, the latter is by far the most fastidious
and dainty and hence more welcome inside my home as a companion.
There must be a reason why dogs are not permitted along with their
owners in most restaurants by the proprietors, whereas the presence of
the café cat stalking about or sitting under a table seems to disturb
no one except the phobes. The cat likes nice smells such as flowers, spices,
perfumes. It also likes nice things to lie on such as silks, satins, or furs. A
healthy cat has no odor, its fur shines. It presents the appearance of a
lady or a gentleman.

Monkeys have no manners at all; people have not very many; cats
have not only manners but, coupled with this, another quality mostly
lacking in man, namely, charity. And the astonishing thing is that the
puss is able to combine both of these on the most difficult level: during
its feeding. A cat will often share its meal with a hungry stranger and
will also, when dining with a friend, wait politely until the other has
finished before proceeding to the dish himself.

The human has learned equal self-restraint and practices hospitality
extended to an invited guest, but said guest is rarely a bum invited in off
the street.

This tolerance on kitty's part presupposes some extraordinary kind
of understanding that the guest is in trouble and in need of a meal and is
not in any way an interloper, of course, or planning to stick around
permanently.

Puss is equally far in the lead with its eating habits. The dog slurps
and gobbles greedily, the monkey scatters its food all over the premises.
The cat goes at its dinner quietly and tidily and what is more exhibits
a trait found in neither of the others and likewise not in humans, that is,
when it has had enough it stops and walks away even should there be
some left in the dish.

And incidentally, speaking of hygiene, there is the little matter of disposal of droppings in which the cat is far ahead of his rivals. The dog is somehow thrilled by what he or any of his friends have produced, hates to leave it, adores smelling it, and sometimes eats it. The monkey is simply disinterested and leaves it where it lies. The cat covers it up if it can.

Again, to be fair, the cat, as you will probably have read, has a particular reason, after eliminating, for going through that ceremony with his two front paws of burying his deposit, and there is nothing more unhappy than the expression on the face of puss when he has been compelled to perform in the street or on some other kind of unyielding substance and he scratches and paws in vain. The action, of course, is inherited from his jungle days when he found it necessary to conceal the scent so as not to advertise his presence to the game he was planning to hunt. However, any way you look at it, it is a smart thing to do.

And finally, while the cat has become a byword for treachery and unreliability, it is the monkey actually who is never wholly to be trusted and even some breeds of man's best friend will suddenly turn and bite the hand that feeds them. Else whence this all too familiar expression?

People who understand cats never get either scratched or bitten. There are only two occasions when biting or scratching are likely to occur: when a cat is in pain, or hurt or frightened, and a sensitive spot is touched, or when, through too much petting or fussing or stomach rubbing, the cat is sexually stimulated. Like humans, cats, when they make love, frequently add to the general enjoyment by biting the lady a little. Most wounds suffered by humans at the hands of cats are self-inflicted. When the excited cat seizes a hand in its paws, the ununderstanding person panics and pulls away; kitty holds on tight. It is the skin that gives. Leave the hand quietly there or give with the pull and no damage will result.

And here, having awarded the palm for the highest animal I.Q. to Felis catus, I leave you either to applaud or to gnash your teeth at such obtuseness and lack of understanding of man's other animal friends. I don't mean to be arbitrary, it's just how it looks to me.

Beauty

IF it is true that beauty lieth in the eye of the beholder then the continuous and manifold appeal of the cat lieth most felicitously in mine and the word comes into its fullest interpretation. Everything a cat is and does physically is to me beautiful, lovely, stimulating, soothing, attractive, and an enchantment.

It begins, I should say, with the compactness of construction, composition, size, proportion, and general overall form. The domesticated

cat is the tidiest of all animals. There is an almost divine neatness and
economy about the animal. Completely packaged in fur with not a bald
spot showing, rarely two specimens wholly alike, it often comes decorated
with designs that Picasso might envy and always functionally streamlined
for every activity; just another case of the practical made glamorous.

I will not deny you that there are beautiful dog faces, some with
expressions that pierce you directly to the heart, but the dog has been
bred into some weirdo sizes and shapes of body, some of which must cause
the poor animal considerable embarrassment. With the cat the arrangement
of eyes, nose, mouth, and ears is superbly drawn to give the utmost
satisfaction to the beholder, and the eyes themselves with their depth
and mystery are deserving of a chapter alone. Nobody has ever managed
to breed the cat into an ugly shape with the possible exception of that
genetic sport the Manx cat, tailless and with its hind legs slightly out
of plumb, reminiscent of the bunny rabbit. One feels sorry for this accident.
To fulfill its definition a cat wants a tail, so that one's eye can travel
easily along its lithe body from the tip of its whiskers to the gracefully
waving appendage.

It is not true to say that there are no ugly cats; there are indeed
occasionally squint-eyed, ill-favored creatures decorated with badly mis-
matched colors and even sometimes misshapen. But if you can put up with
the paradox, to me, as the animal still remains a cat, it still retains its
measure of beauty. Furthermore it doesn't know it is ugly and thus my heart
goes out to it. Also, its mother loves it.

Except for the bright-plumaged birds, the cat surpasses all specimens
of the animal kingdom including, I must add, ourselves, in the variety
of hues and design.

It all began as protective coloration and jungle camouflage, and your
tabby still persists in the stripes that were developed to make it invisible
against thickets and bamboos and reeds. The wall paintings of the Egyptian
cats show this pattern to predominate.

But down through some four thousand years from B.C. to A.D. the cat
by natural selection must have been preparing itself for modern times and
modern eyes in shades and patterns. To the pure white and the almost
totally black (you know, of course, that there is no such thing as a wholly
black cat; you always find at least a few white hairs on his chest to keep
it out of the hands of the witches) are now added the ginger, the red
tabby, the café-au-lait Siamese with its eyes of exquisite translucent blue
shining from a black mask, the grays, the silvers, the browns and blues,
and the surrealistic mixtures of the calico cat as well as other crazy-quilt
numbers resulting from some of the more casual adventures in love.

Plato characterized beauty by measure and symmetry, Plotinus as being
the supremacy of the higher over the lower, of form and matter, and
Cicero, as distinguished from the useful and compromising as distinct
types of dignity and charm and grace. Old Noah Webster dissects the
word *beauty* as an assemblage of graces or properties or some one of them

satisfactory to the eye, the intellect, the aesthetic faculty, and the moral sense; also abstract quality characteristic of such properties.

But Mr. Webster, who may never have owned a cat, leaves out "touch," important to any definition and which, however, is included among the sensuous qualities. Oh, yes, there is no question but what the fur of the cat is pleasing to touch and, circa the turn of the century, therapeutic to bronchial troubles when worn next to the skin on the chest, separated, however, from the cat before applying. It is more than pleasing, namely alluring, seductive, and irresistible, the latter in the sense that if you are not a phobe, it is almost impossible *not* to stroke a cat that comes within range.

Humans, like the monkey, are all touchers; we need to receive messages tactilely through the ends of our fingers, and one of the most pleasurable of such communications is between cat and oneself as one passes one's hand over its sleek body. I believe the psychiatrists lift an eyebrow at this and mutter something about sexual connotations which I am not prepared to argue since sex can be beautiful too. Soft is good. And when the cat pushes its firm but delicate little skull wrapped in softness, as it were, against the heel of our hand, the effect is delightful; and sometimes, as a grace note, like pepper and salt added to a fine dish, the cat fur crackles with electricity and bestows the bonus of a fine tingle to our fingers.

I consider few sounds more gratifying than a purr, unless it be that divine melody sung by a happy feline which combines both a purr and a little cry, the well-known "Prrrrrrrrr-mow!"

The purr is an indescribable sound, and this forced combination of letters, namely "prrrrrr," does it no justice. One can only refer to the sense of joy and tranquility experienced by the purrer and transferred to the soul of the listener. There are times, though regrettably not too many, when we ourselves would purr if we could. Yet, with all our faculties, we simply have no way of expressing our completest satisfaction with the moment to compare with that of House Cat.

The purr is beautiful! I doubt whether it could be properly reproduced, say, even by the most delicate electronic recorder. It would come out as some other kind of noise since the machine's mechanical heart simply would be unable to reproduce all the internal vibrations provided by the contentment of the cat, and our human ear would very quickly detect the counterfeit.

I will admit that there is nothing harmonious or attractive about a catfight. But the back fence nighttime melody of wooing has its moment, provided you are not an irritable person dead bent on getting to sleep. The appeal lies in its primitiveness and naturalness. Surely all men at some time when they have been in love have wished that they might sing to the object thereof, to pour forth under her window the fullness and the glory of the emotion she has aroused in them. One is aware that if one did one would be cutting a ridiculous figure, nor would the noises emerging from one's throat do the trick.

Not so the cat. When so moved, he simply sings and his lady loves it.

When the earth was very young and the antediluvian carnivores were

a-prowl, the endless savannas of the wilderness must have echoed to such
music. Something in our ears and hearts can remember it.

Again with the aesthetic faculty appealed to, beauty offers the combination of the sublime, the tragic, and the comic. The cat offers me all three, present either singly or in combination. Sublime is an empyrean word, but there are moments when the cat is entitled to it, for there are few expressions that can match those on the face of Mother House Cat as she tends her young, or presents them, or even prepares for delivery. And as for the tragic, you will have to seek far for a greater sadness, gallantry, and nobility than that of a long-time friend, an old cat at its dying. A starving, ill-treated specimen has the power to arouse our sympathies almost to the extent of that of a cruelly treated child. For all the pampering that accrues to the lucky one, cats in a sense are waifs in the world, each and every one a candidate for adoption. Those that fail to achieve it are the tragic figures.

And withal, and still within the definition of beauty, the comic is never far from the surface of the animal. Cats are funny. They have always appealed to humorists, cartoonists, and poets.

A cat's comedy is unconscious, slightly rueful, and often delicate. You have only to make the egregious error of laughing out loud, instead of enjoying the moment inwardly, to destroy it. You will also insult your cat almost beyond redemption and it will be days before you are forgiven; it cannot bear to be laughed *at*. But you must not mind if its sense of humor manifests itself in taking advantage of your own weaknesses, foibles, or inability to measure up.

Cats don't laugh; they do grin as anyone familiar with Lewis Carroll and *Alice* knows, but even the grin of the Cheshire Cat, and for that matter any cat, is suspect since it may be an expression connected with something quite different, such as the various emotions ascribed to a baby because of that look that comes over its face just before it is about to be untidy.

But the cat definitely has its funny moments, even almost up to the point of near-hysteria, when it suddenly seems to go mad and flies all over the premises, up and down curtains, in and around and over furniture at high speeds, only to stop suddenly, look around at you with an expression that may be accurately determined as "Hasn't this been a lark?" The cat that decides not to come in at night and leads you on a nocturnal chase you know is laughing its head off at you every time you grab and miss, and the madder you get, the more successful the joke.

But as I have said, you must not return the compliment. If your cat gets itself entangled in something, or falls over while washing or can't get its Ping-Pong ball from under the couch, do, for the sake of a harmonious household, keep a straight face. I have encountered clown cats who wanted to be the center of attraction and who didn't mind that you shouted with laughter at their antics, but this type most definitely lets us know. It is the unconscious and basic gaiety of the cat that verges on beauty.

And so finally to the last word connected with the formal beauty of these animals, namely their attitudes. Attitudes and poses! The former are natural, the latter deliberate. There are, for instance, all the various positions for washing, too well known to be redescribed, but there are several in particular which come to my mind such as when the cat swivels its head almost ninety degrees on its neck and then with long sweeping strokes works its long tongue down over its shoulders and spine. And what movement is more charming than that in which the side of the paw is moistened and then rubbed vigorously over an ear?

An attitude need not be static. A cat running is a flow of rhythm and coordination which, in a moment, can be turned to the most amusing burlesque when it decides to gallop and bring its padded feet down hard upon the floor. Or is there any lazier or more luxurious movement than a cat getting up and stretching? Always, always, is the eye diverted and the intellect of appreciation stimulated by movement. House Cat jumping, pouncing, playing, rolling, cruising; each of these has its moments of supreme delectation. Nothing the animal does is ungraceful.

But I think a cat at rest with me in the same room is what I like best. The curl-up in a perfect circle or sometimes with one paw over its eyes as though to shut out the light; the hunker with all four feet tidily tucked under, or the sit-up with its tail neatly tucked around its bottom. The poses I know are sheer vanity, for cats are indeed vain and like to be admired. But they will choose backgrounds and put themselves into positions which they know are admirable. They will drape their bodies to the shape of a piece of furniture. They will hang a paw in what seems to be a wholly casual manner, but you know and they know damn well that it is studied. But it is never wrong. Merely by the turn of their heads upon their necks, a half an inch or so, they can change the picture and give expression to some inner feeling and, by doing so, set up a glow of appreciation in the watcher.

Well, and as for words, they define less than House Cat illustrates them: aesthetic, sublime, tragic, comic; symmetry, supremacy, dignity, charm and grace; in short, the beautiful.

Are Cats Womany, and Vice Versa

THE question as to whether one cat might say to another, "Now don't be womany, dear," might give rise to some fruitful examination. The phrase of comparison that women are "catty" has been accepted for so long that no one has thought to question it. I do.

There are areas of resemblance between the female of the two species, but I maintain that the implications that lie behind the above are not valid. Let us examine the bromide.

A lady makes a denigrating remark about another, in all probability her best friend. The remark may be true or untrue, justified or unjustified, prompted by envy, jealousy, spite, or the desire to be thought clever. This is lumped under the term "cattiness." But what has this to do with the nature and behavior of the cat?

"Aha," you will say, "the lady is being false, sly, cruel, vicious, two-faced, and untrustworthy." Miaow! Yet your parlor kitty is none of these and not even the accepted tenets as to its cruelty will stand up as I will show in another chapter.

Basically cats are not false. They are great kidders, conners, and flatterers; characteristics they make no effort to conceal. But you will remember that at no time have they ever promised you unto death a return for what you are bestowing upon them. You cannot ever accuse them of a double cross. They may give you all—loyalty, faithfulness, affection—but there is no contract to that effect and if you truly understand the nature of your pet you will not expect more than it is prepared to deliver. You live with your cat on two different levels. While its care and comfort is binding upon you, the cat, as said before, has signed no documents.

The human female, however, when she is being "catty" is actually being merely human. We are known to be often disloyal, treacherous, unreliable, selfish, double-crossing—liars and breakers of promises. We have the unique ability to work deliberate woe upon those we are affecting to love. Most of these depressing traits are demonstrated by speech, for it is largely through talk that we deceive. Until you manage to achieve communication with your cat to the point where it tells you one thing and does another, you have weakened if not utterly destroyed your case, by calling a woman's remarks "catty."

Cats scratch. They get their claws into you. Women "show their claws" and have been known to use their fingernails for more than a base for polish. And once more the house cat bears the brunt of the insult. Come, come, monkeys both scratch and bite and usually without either warning or provocation. So do birds of prey and various other animals equipped to do so. Claws and sharp nails at the business end of hands and feet are not restricted to the *Felidae*.

But if the cat were brought into court on charges of using his hands in the manner of a woman, a competent attorney would very soon demolish the case against his client. For a cat doesn't scratch in the sense and meaning that we have given the word, and more often than not when it is parked in your lap and digs its spikes into your legs, you are not suffering a clawing in that interpretation. On the contrary, the animal is paying you the highest compliment of which it is capable, namely to be reminded by the pleasure of your company of its happiest moments as a kitten, when feeding, it would work its mother's breast and teats with its paws to increase the flow of milk. You have fallen victim to nothing more sinister than reverse psychology. The kneading motion has become associated with happiness. Contentment has triggered it. You have made a hit and can afford to suffer a little for it.

I will concede that when a lady gets something desirable such as a man or an article into her claws or clutches she will hang on like grim death. The cat uses its own holding apparatus to the same purpose, the retractile nails taking the place of fingers for grasping. The mechanism in one sense resembles the barbed fishhook with the incidence of curve and angle of holding all in favor of the cat. The action is almost automatic. A woman has no such reflex machinery. When she lets you have her nails, it is deliberate.

Furthermore, your counsel will demonstrate that when your or somebody else's pet cat uses its war hooks it has a legitimate reason and one which the scratchee in his or her omnipotence has overlooked. We forget the vast difference in our sizes and that we must loom over puss often as most monstrous giants of unlimited power, not to mention, frequently of not wholly attractive odor. Cats become upset by people whose bodies or souls are sometimes less than fragrant. Cats like perfume, too, and are grateful to the wearer.

Or, outweighing the cat by a ratio of say, twenty to one, we play too rough to the point where fun suddenly becomes menace and, before we know it, the sacred blood of the great gods that we are has been shed.

Immediately the blame is put upon the cat. "Why you double-crossing little beast." Charge ourselves? Never.

No, the claws and scratch comparison won't wash, by and large. Nor will the accusation of slyness and "Sly Puss" is an overworked cliché. Cats are the most straightforward and forthcoming animals in the entire kingdom. They manage at all times to let you know exactly what they want and what is on their minds. Women expect you to guess what is on theirs and become aggrieved when you don't. A cat doesn't linger over making its desires known. A woman will wait for days, letting you hang yourself by your continued ignorance and insensitivity and then let you know just how long she has been nurturing a desire which you have failed to fathom.

But why must all comparisons fall to the debit side between puss and wife or sweetheart? There are several ways in which they *do* resemble one another, but these are all to the good and should be encouraged and perpetuated.

Cat's eyes in the face of a woman, particularly when half-closed and slightly slanted upward. seem to promise the most unusual and selective delights as green and seductive they glitter behind narrowed slits. Oh, give me your cat-eyed woman and I will follow slavishly in her train.

But there is more to it than just the eyes. The cat face is an ensemble of marvelously matched and balanced features and the total result is one to stir the heart. Where the human female is able to approach them, she becomes irresistible. How often have I thought when looking into the face of a particularly beautiful or expressive cat, *Ah, if you were but a woman I should like to court and marry you.* Aesop made this longing the basis of a Pygmalion-like fable of the young man who prayed to Venus to change *his* cat into a woman so that he could do just that. The goddess obliged, and the chap enjoyed what promised to be bliss unalloyed, until unfortunately an alloy did develop. The lady could not be broken of the habit of leaping out of bed and pouncing upon mice that appeared out of the wainscoting, and so the delicious experiment had to be reversed. But there is no doubt in my mind that the fellow had the right idea.

But come, we are not yet done with the brighter side of speculation on the affinity. Why do we think of or even call a particularly cuddly specimen of the female of our species "Kitten"? Exactly. Because she is delectable, soft, pettable; sufficiently diminutive to curl up into our laps, or snuggle close to us in bed, and because everything about her aspect, her fragrance, and her touch is pleasing and charming. There is hardly a higher compliment in the area of personal aspect that you could bestow upon her.

And finally there is the matter of the essential mystery inherent in woman and cat. No one ever really understands either or manages wholly to part the veil.

Man may speculate, but he cannot ever be wholly certain, and therein lies the charm, excitement, and attraction. It is just as possible to misjudge the depth of a woman as it is to interpret certain expressions on the face of the house feline. Some ladies who can turn up the corners of their lovely mouths in that secret feline smile of introspective communing with the ages may be abysmally stupid, but the expression itself is totally alluring, and as to what might lie behind it or not one can never be sure that she isn't just pretending to be stupid to make her man feel wise.

I for one am not inclined to pry too closely. Both cat and woman have legitimate pretensions to the divine and the mysteries connected with this branch of relationship. The former has had the experience of being worshipped as a god, the latter as a goddess and it has left its mark upon them and, too, upon us males—cat and woman lovers.

How Cruel Are Cats?

OF course, the grand joke in discussing the much referred to "cruelty" of house or barn cat at work is the inclusion of the word "inhuman" in its list of synonyms, namely, "harshness, brutality, ruthlessness, barbarity, inhumanity, atrocity."

The case immediately collapses and kitty is entitled to laugh its head off every time it hears the word applied to itself, what it does, and how. For cruelty is one of the specialties of the human, since it is with deliberation, forethought, and the knowledge that we are indifferent to or, in the definition of the word, disposed to take pleasure in the pain or distress of another, or to show ourselves hardhearted and pitiless. We know better and yet have remained specialists in the practice thereof.

The charges brought against the cat are based purely upon observation of its hunting tactics. This and the fact that it includes birds among its prey: the reputation of the cat has suffered mostly from the highly vocal lobby of the bird lovers. And once again it is necessary to point out that bird lovers are people. Worms, fish, insects, frogs, snakes, and small rodents that are attacked by birds, carried off, mangled horribly, and then eaten are not exactly included among the worshippers of our feathered friends.

It all boils down rather to who eats whom. Since the bird lover will sit down to a tasty dish of partridge, quail or pheasant while his heart bleeds for the sparrow, the robin, or the linnet which is less edible, the situation is likely to become confused. One thing, however, is certain; if you separate the word *cruelty* from deliberate intent and consider only results, the bird is as cruel as the cat and, furthermore, is one up in that it can attack via another dimension.

"Like a cat playing with a mouse!" You know that phrase. Falsely worded. It should be—like a cat "practicing" or "training" with a mouse.

Gentlemen hunters used to practice their skill with wing shots using live pigeons released from a trap until the advent of the clay disk that serves the same purpose. Before we became aware that we were destroying all wild animal life in our presence, game was shot for the fun of it and to increase one's efficiency, rather than for the pot.

The cat is a hunter for food and the instinct has never been bred out of it. Games with an injured prey have nothing to do with the will to cause it pain or suffering. There are two main objectives; to keep the hunting muscles and speed and timing sharp, or to bring a no longer dangerous specimen to its kittens for similar exercises. As to the latter tactic, one remembers that the picadors injure the bull before he is turned over to the mercies of the brave matador.

Almost all of a cat's "play" is not play at all, but practice. Its immediate interest in anything small that moves, a leaf, a blade of grass stirred by the wind, a flutter of paper, a thistledown, is reflex. If it moves it may be alive, if alive and small it may be catchable and edible.

There are the hunter and the hunted and let the hunted beware in the inexorable hierarchy of Nature. The cat stalking the field mouse in the meadow should not forget the eagle or the goshawk hovering in the sky.

But let us confine ourselves to the mouse which has its own endowments of speed, scent, cunning, and instinct and is often smart enough to move himself and his family out of the house when cat moves in. Try getting down on your elbows and knees to catch a mouse with your bare hands. You won't, but if you should succeed, you are likely to get bitten and, if it should be a rat, you might die of the bite. Well, we are smarter and know our limitations. We invent and set a trap for the mouse, treacherously baited with its favorite dish. The spring trap if it does not hit just the right angle lets the mouse linger at its dying all through the night.

The cat has to work it all on its own, with skill, concealment, judgment of distance, and speed. It must strike like lightning. Have you watched your cat, as you trail a piece of paper tied to string across the floor, waggle its bottom before it pounces? The boxer, the fencer, the football, baseball, and tennis player have all learned that one moves more quickly out of movement than from the stationary.

Infinite patience, perfect timing are involved in a successful mouse hunt; savvy, planning, plus absolute muscular control.

But at no time is the cat emotionally involved with the mouse. It has neither knowledge of nor interest in how the mouse feels about it. Nor are there that many mice about, nor does the cat always win. There are fast and savvy mice too. Thus, one caught and not wholly disabled by the first pounce becomes a valuable prize and training adjunct. But sheer thoughtless, heedless, or planned and intended cruelty as we know of it today, by our own standards, is no part of the picture. Even a tree may suffer agonies when it is cut down. We have no way of knowing, and if we did, we would still cut down trees.

A bird, is a bird, is a bird, as it might have appeared to the late Miss Stein, but to a cat it is a meal and not only a meal but the superchallenge. The fact that it sings beautifully doesn't interfere with its flavor, or that soaring in the heavens or perched on a leafy branch it is a delight to the eye. The cat would never understand the practice of keeping such a dinner caged during its lifetime.

It might even consider this to come under the head of that mysterious word used so lightly by humans—"cruelty."

They See through Us

COMPOSING these particular thoughts as one male to another instead of addressed to the whole human race, I will commence by saying that if you are a married man you will suspect that your wife sees through you; you will know that your dog doesn't; you will hope that your children don't, but you can bet all the little red books in China that your cat does. Can you bear it? And if not, what are you doing with a cat in the house anyway?

I am not prepared to so much as hazard a guess as to how a cat feels toward a woman, since I am neither. Perhaps woman's mystique goes some distance toward canceling out that of the cat. Neither intrudes upon the other's secrets. But where men, their patron lords, are concerned, cats most definitely have and maintain the upper hand. They have our number. Also, except when it suits their convenience or intentions, they refuse to subscribe to the fiction that we are masters in our own homes, much less elsewhere.

This demands either that we come equipped with hides like a rhinoceros's to our nervous systems, or are emotionally and psychologically equipped to put up with somewhat less than total adulation.

The cat, therefore, is not for the pompous, the conceited, the stuffed shirt, or the unmitigated tyrant. Nor is this animal too desirable for the individual with a psychic leakage, lack of self-confidence, or a bleeding inferiority complex. The former, exposed to the behavior of puss, will be permanently offended, the latter equally permanently hurt.

It is on this level of relationship to the nominal head of the house that the domesticated cat and dog differ so greatly.

The dog offers visible signs of worship at any time of night or day. Many dog owners both need and accept this perpetual approbation as their due. The cat maintains a constant reserve and doles out its favors sparingly. This puts a greater price and value upon these favors and the cat man is therefore the more gratified and uplifted upon receipt.

The dog seems to be the natural venerator of the human species. At some stage of his development it became contented to have a bone tossed to it at the fireside. The cat has always been prepared to go out and work for its own bone. The dog who is taken into the home has no problems. The cat has, having a mind of its own which on many levels diverges sharply from that of The Great Provider, including the matter of house rules. You can tell your dog to go to his corner/basket/blanket/ place and lie down and it will obey. Try that on your cat.

For puss to create for itself a comfortable life in your home according to its needs and desires, not to mention whims, it is necessary for it to evaluate the members of the family with whom it lives. This calls for unusual perspicacity and psychological insight. But this is exactly what I am warning you the cat has and every prospective host to one of them must be prepared to take the consequences.

Husband or wife may consider himself or herself ruler of the roost, but the cat will unerringly divine and know who is and play its cards accordingly. When there is a sense of humor present among the humans, this will work no damage. But stiff necks and cats don't go together, and there will be no contentment in an establishment where such prevail.

Fortunately, the chances are that very few people who oughtn't to have a cat are likely to want or acquire one. The person whose heart goes out to a lonely, hungry, and not too attractive-looking stray and who picks one up off the street and adopts it is obviously the right kind of human being. So is the one who falls for one of the grocer's kittens or, in passing a pet shop window, receives waves of a silent and irresistible summons. The ailurophobe will shy away from the species automatically, as will the psychologically unfit. And as to those whose personalities clash, the error soon enough becomes apparent and in time for parting company without too much damage to the *amour propre* of either.

You must get used to being looked at or contemplated by your cat occasionally without inquiring into, or caring about, what it is thinking. This is the best way. But if speculation leads you to self-analysis and even self-incrimination as you ponder on what you might have done wrong to man or beast that day, or particularly to kitty, why there is no great harm in that and the effect could be quite salutary. One's wife knows the gambit. Silence, tight lips. The hurt look. Eventually you are compelled to ask, "What's the matter, darling?" to receive that first inevitable reply, "Oh, nothing!" which then leads you on to press the matter to disaster; the revelation of your crime.

The cat is committed to silence and you to your imagination.

Disdain is an important weapon in the armory of the pet cat and if you cannot put up with this, you'd better not have one.

We are, no matter how adult and civilized, incorrigible givers of bounty. We invented the saying "It is more blessed to give than to receive" less as a Sunday school tract to discipline the young than as an acknowledgment of how good it makes us feel to give a handout of any kind.

God gives, or at least we are always importuning Him to do so, and when we give no matter what, a small present, a large one, food, trinkets, surprises or whatever, it makes us feel for the moment godlike. Naturally, house cat knows and hence works this lode to the utmost.

Besides, giving, too, is a form of bribery. The giver, even if sometimes the sense is infinitesimal, is always hoping that the recipient will love him or her just a little more for the gift. Kitty knows this and if it doesn't it will find out very soon. So here you have your cat working you on two fronts and this is why it is so difficult to resist its demands. It has read you like a book and got you coming and going.

Besides which there is a third point of attack, namely that over the centuries of vicissitudes and experience with the human race, the cat has learned to take it or leave it without going into a sulk or bearing the kind of grudge that lets you off the hook by stimulating you to reprisals. It has gambits far more effective. When it panhandles you for a tidbit at the table, in itself a gesture usually prohibited (and the rule most often broken) and you refuse, it will either accept it philosophically and put it down to the fact that you have had a bad day at the office, or favor you with a look of deep disappointment and walk away with every attitude of its body expressing the evaluation—"cheapskate!" If you know and understand these ploys you can also learn to put up with them without too much loss of self-respect.

A cat that dislikes certain foods will let you know very quickly by not eating them. You aren't going to let your pet starve, so you experiment with what it *does* enjoy and thus your education progresses to the point where you learn which expensive delicacies will send your friend into absolute ecstasies of delight. Thereby having learned what is the treat supreme, you again approach the godlike element. By withholding it, you can also work up a pretty good guilt complex.

Your cat will present to you the problem of the door it cannot operate itself and so asks you to let it out. You are busy or out of sorts, or just not in the mood to act as footman to an animal, so you ignore the request as a part of the "goddam-cat-is-always-on-the-wrong-side-of-the-door" syndrome. Well, after a time House Cat simply postpones its outing or whatever it had in mind to do and goes off and does something else. And if it was a full bladder that was calling for the outing, it simply holds it like a gentleman. But pretty soon you find yourself feeling like a first-class heel. What I am driving at is that the cat knows its owner must be basically a good guy. Therefore, whenever it is able to make him feel like a baddy, it wins.

Good guys are just as subject to flattery as fools, and there is nothing wrong with this as long as we are aware of it. If the human can dole out his treats, so can pussy with its moments of affection, uninspired by the contents of the cupboard. It doesn't spoil its owners.

These are practical things which anyone who has been associated with the cat as a house pet will know and copes with to the best of his or her ability, which makes for a peaceful and happy association. By the same token, one learns very quickly when one has insulted one's cat, hurt its feelings by laughing at it, and disappointed it by doing something stupid or careless to it. Kitty knows how to punish, either by retiring under the bed or chiffonier or stalking about the house with an injured look on its face, refusing to be mollified and simply averting its head when cajoled, or washing vigorously when advances are made to it, as a means of letting you know it is not to be bothered. A magnanimous animal, eventually it forgives you, though it may not forget.

But eventually it all comes back to what I was hinting at in the beginning, and that is my conviction that our cat knows a great deal more about us than it is telling and has penetrated much further into our innermost secrets and psyche than we even suspect.

Is our cat our conscience? Did the ancient Egyptians know something when they made of it a god and sent garlanded maidens and musicians dancing about its altar and meted out death to anyone who injured or killed a cat? Has it really occult powers of divination, prophecy, or communication with the unknown as was believed in past centuries? Was there a reason for the long-time association of the black cat and the witch and the linking of the cat with the devil? From god to Beelzebub to household pet. That takes some doing.

Delving into the history of this remarkable animal turns up many a strange tale of their necromantic powers. Pish and tosh and ignorant superstition, but also no smoke without fire, eh?

For instance take their manner of communication. It ought to be very worrying to us moderns who believe ourselves to be standing on the threshold of solving some of the mysteries of the unknown. The cat invented radar and extrasensory perception long before we ever thought of it. Nobody has ever heard a cat "miaow" to or at another cat. They shout and yell and scream when preparing for battle, but they don't "talk" audibly to one another. Their little cries are reserved for us. Yet somehow either through the antennae of their whiskers, or pure thought broadcasters and receivers, they are attuned to one another and know what is going on.

And if they can do this, what is to prevent them from penetrating our thoughts—if not now, then eventually? I have always been just a little wary of letting cats know too much about my business, and I have encountered people who when talking before their cat and working on the theory that it cannot spell will say, "Did you put the l-o-b-s-t-e-r in the f-r-i-d-g-e?" This because they suspect, if they do not know, that the cat has mastered the mechanics of opening and shutting the food safe.

But, of course, this is ridiculous and I don't mean to imply that my cat reads my mail or listens in to my telephone conversations or catches me fantasizing in a sticky manner the elimination of someone who is irritating me, but I wouldn't put it past it. Sometimes when I am aware that I have suddenly come under the silent and analyzing scrutiny, I attempt quickly to foil it by envisioning a blank wall, let us say, or a cloudless sky, or an empty blue sea stretching to the horizon; anything to keep it from penetrating that weak, foolish, vain fellow who is myself.

Why then, you might ask, should I expose myself to such semimagical penetration and examination? Why should you, or anyone? Why do people keep cats?

The only answer I can offer you is that the price is not too high to pay. The fact that all the cats with whom I have lived in the past have read me and having found me not too unbearable have consented to remain as guests in my house and that *they* have not found the cost too high has been sufficiently flattering to me. But I do think, perhaps immodestly, that it calls for a rather well-adjusted and unshakable character to accept this.

We, the Chosen

QUIETLY over the recent years one has become aware of a new and active cult appearing upon the scene, stimulated in part by such writings as those of Colette, Michael Joseph, Compton Mackenzie, T. S. Eliot, Beverley Nichols and others, and perhaps even some guilt coming my way, namely not so much the cult of the cat but a rather more terrifying one, the cult of what we, in an onset of preciousness, refer to as "Cat People."

"Cat People," when they discover one another either by confession or the telltale presence of cat hairs upon their clothing, are apt to rush hysterically into one another's arms with little shrieks of joy, embrace like long-lost relatives and recognize immediately that they are set apart from other mortals. Or they will instantly retire from the middle of any gathering off to a corner to exchange anecdotes. The attitude is one of having found a fraternity brother or sorority sister, one more member of the elite outstanding in a world of Yahoos. Dearly beloved friends and fellow cat lovers, I notice to my distress that we are becoming self-congratulatory and standing in the greatest peril of becoming a group of thundering bores.

It has sort of crept up on us quietly and we have been seduced partly by the spate of cat anthologies which have invariably included a chapter on celebrities past and present who have been devotees of cats. This list includes some really luscious names with which I admit it is a pleasure to be associated: emperors, kings, queens, grand viziers and prime ministers, statesmen, generals, conquerors, great painters, writers, musicians, actors and actresses, a certain cream-of-the-crop who have either left a thumbprint on the pages of history or are always being photographed or written up in the daily press.

The operative syllogism might read, "Some of the world's greatest celebrities have loved cats; we love cats; therefore we are like some of the world's greatest celebrities." This fits so neatly with our psychic needs that we are tempted to forget that there must be a great number of famous people who have loathed cats and wouldn't have one around the house at any price. If we were at all to preen ourselves at possessing the superior characteristics of cat lovers, we must also be fair.

Actually one notices the tendency to equate cat worshippers and non-cat lovers almost with the goodies and the baddies. We are beginning to wear our white Stetsons with an air of pious arrogance, sniffing audibly in the presence of a black-hatted, dyed-in-the-wool phobe or even those prepared to admit casually that they can take cats or leave them alone.

And so without any organization I note with deep misgivings that a kind of club is forming itself. All clubs of any kind are to be decried. The moment we select ourselves, or permit ourselves to be selected, we are abandoning graciousness. You will note that in this discussion and warning I am including myself, for with the preparation of this volume and during a period of self-searching I find I have committed every sin against which I have taken to the pulpit. So there is no use in pointing a finger and crying, "Ya, ya! You do it! In fact you've been one of the worst." Oh, I have, I have, *mea culpa!*

I am, of course, aware that there are perfectly legitimate cat clubs and organizations devoted to the breeding as well as the protection of the more underprivileged and unhappy members of the species. But this is something else again, a private matter that exists due to the fact that cats are with us by the millions because of our own need, desire, or toleration for and of them and hence cannot be ignored.

The group that is beginning to worry me are those of us who enjoy pointing out that we are special and quite different from dog lovers and that so well adjusted are we, and perhaps so coolly cognizant of the nature of our own worth, that we don't need the flattery and worship of an animal to bolster up our egos. This is the base of the schism with the dog lover upon whom we look down as someone slightly less strong and not as finely balanced as ourselves, a creature who needs the applause of a wagging tail. But if there is anything more tiresome than listening to tales of the accomplishments of somebody else's cat, it is having to listen to the performances of their children, accompanied by photographs.

And is there more to it perhaps than just enjoying the fraternity of affection for one certain animal? If not, why is there no meetinghouse for the worshippers of hippopotamuses (who actually in ancient Egypt *were* once holy), no organization of lovers of the shy okapi, a mysterious and only recently discovered relative of the giraffe, and no one to sympathize with the unloved hyena?

No other animal has managed to get itself tangled up in as much legend, myth, symbolism, religion, history, and human affairs as the cat. From the time it first appeared upon the scene some four thousand years ago, it has played its part in almost every age. And indeed, one of the

chief and yet unsolved mysteries connected with this animal is that before
the earliest Egyptian dynasties and wall decorations, there is no record of
this animal at all, neither in cave art or kitchen middens. It is as though it
suddenly appeared on earth, neatly packaged and with all its qualities,
practically as we know it today.

Are we, as its devotees, hoping that some of this marvel and mystery
will rub off on us by cultivating it and thus elevate us a cut above the
rest of the herd?

Black magic, white magic, good luck and bad, a hundred superstitions
covering every aspect of human life and condition, are ascribed to the cat.
It became the familiar of witches, the companion of the devil and, of
course, a god in its own right.

Here is a compendium to attract mere mortals, and what is more there
is a magic about it overall, and what we would dearly love to be is magi-
cians with supernatural powers. The cat would have seemed to have
retained some of these occult faculties. Let us therefore be friends to them
and friends of their friends.

Yet we must remember that for all the superiority we arrogate to
ourselves through acknowledging that we are the elect who know how to
appreciate the cat, we remain on the outside looking in, at a society to
which we are never admitted on anything like an equal footing. The cat
has never subscribed to any such thing as a cult of People Lovers and I
would guess doesn't even discuss us during a backyard conference.

In fact, and this ought to shrink our hat sizes, the brute frequently
even disdains to recognize and pay proper due to the acknowledged cat
person. I can only illustrate this with a humiliating experience of mine
and one of my most embarrassing moments which occurred many years
ago when because of a novel I had produced in which the main characters
were cats, I was invited to lunch with a member of the British Royal
Family and her children, with whom this animal was a favorite.

After the repast we all trooped down to the barn for the ultimate
moment where the family pet and prize specimen, a burly black and white
Tom, was to be introduced to one who from his writings was suspected
of having been a cat in another incarnation.

It never dawned on me that I might not pass the test. Wasn't I a full-
fledged "cat person"? Hadn't I cozened, cosseted, spoiled, pampered,
housed and boarded them wholesale?

Tom was put into my arms and while the Personage and her brood
watched waiting for the manifestation of affinity and love at first sight, the
animal spit in my eye, raked my cheek, tore himself squalling from my
embrace, and went and hid under something.

After first aid, I departed, leaving behind me an unquestionable air of
suspicion that false pretenses had been involved and that I was some kind
of fake who obviously had been unmasked by their pet and had been
given his just deserts for the imposture. At any rate, I was never asked back.

A television show I once participated in with the actress Lili Palmer
involving a cat and the poem by William Blake, "Tiger, Tiger, Burning

Bright," turned into a public catastrophe because the miniature tiger loaned to the studio failed to return my glow, though it revealed its superior intelligence by showing no objection to Lili. It had simply formed an opinion of me at the outset of the program and didn't care that some ten million viewers shared it.

Come to think of it, I can hardly ever remember having a cat handed to me to hold for purposes of publicity photography that the animal did not immediately set up a frantic struggle to get away, with none of my professional blandishments prevailing. The perverse little bastards merely increase their efforts to flee, with the ensuing glossy prints revealing the struggle or the fact that I am triumphing only by main force.

Yet I have had my share of sudden affection from strays and cats of friends, including that head-turning accolade, "Why, kitty seems to like you. She doesn't make friends with everybody." But the point of it all is that you never know.

I have printed the above addressed to "We, the Chosen" in perhaps a futile attempt to curb our arrogance and to point out that there is considerable self-election involved in which the cat cannot be said to have cooperated. If it will help me give up the retailing of dull catecdotes and trying to impress others with the superiority supposedly conferred upon me by my weakness for the common house cat, it will come under the head of a public service.

Strays

IS there a more pitiable creature in the realm of four-footed animals than the stray cat, foodless, shelterless, harried through the back alleys and slums of the cities of the world?

The lost or abandoned dog of the streets, searching with haunted eyes into human faces for someone who will be friend and master again, wrings the heart too. But how dare one think of beasts as long as there is still a single child in the world, its body clad in rags, its stomach distended by starvation, its limbs maimed, orphaned or abandoned, staring its silent reproach at one from page or flickering screen?

And yet somehow it is the homeless cat that has become the byword for misery and wretchedness and which daily holds up the mirror to human conscienceless neglect of all that suffer.

And so this derelict impinges upon my awareness, because it is there. I see it daily, gaunt, bedraggled, dirty, its ribs showing through matted fur, sores on its body and eyes, hungry, frightened, defeated, and it breaks my heart.

It is cold when I am warm, starving when I am sated, wet and shivering in the rain and hail when I am dry and safe, abandoned when I am afforded love and companionship. Nothing softens or ameliorates its life of hardship and squalor: its birthplace and burial ground a refuse heap.

It is, I think, the fall from high estate that makes its plight so vivid and painful. For by nature it is fastidious, gregarious, clean, neat, dignified, and proud.

And it is just that fastidiousness brought into the gutter that weighs upon me, I suppose because in acquiring this quality on our journey up-ward we have kinship with the cats. They are unhappy in the presence of dirt, bad smells, and corruption. Is it perhaps that we can see ourselves, condemned by misfortune to such a life where for sustenance we might have to nose through garbage pails and offal disposal? One is never so high that one cannot be brought low, and the stray produces for us a picture of the depths.

I hear someone cry to a child, "Don't touch that cat! Can't you see it is filthy and sick?" How that beast has need of that touch denied.

And what is it that has separated the shivering bundle of misery huddled beneath a car or fleeing pell-mell over some backyard fence from the sleek and contented beast warming itself at my fireside, clean, fat, sweet smelling, and tidy, its four feet neatly tucked beneath its shining body? Luck!

For every one of these animals upon whom Luck has smiled, a thousand have been passed by and sometimes the passage was so close that only a breath, a partition of a second, a passing footfall separated it from rescue.

And so sometimes I look at my house-friend on the hearth or sitting upon my desk and think, *Do not be too proud or smug, for somewhere your counterpart is dragging itself through wretched days and nights to oblivion because Luck has passed it by, and for those hidden in the dark-ness beyond the lights of our windows there is no justice. Let you and me praise our Luck.*

The Mixed Blessing or Not Entirely Honorable Us

ONE might call this an essay into examination with no intent to be didactic. Superficial, if you will, but in quest of perhaps a few scattered crumbs of truth to be discovered about living with cats and vice versa.

One of these truths which I would put forward is that living with a cat can be something of a mixed blessing. A candid and articulate cat would probably admit to the same. Let us then with as much honesty as possible confess these shortcomings and speak up for the cat and its countercharges. And so for us, though we greatly enjoy their company, frankly, there are times when puss is a damned nuisance. Looked upon from the other side of the fence, house cat is perfectly entitled to charge that in our treatment of and behavior toward it we are frequently less than honorable and often heedlessly thoughtless.

I am confining my thoughts and remarks to the urban or apartment cat. Keeping a cat boxed in a set of rooms on the eighth floor is easy neither upon the keeper nor the kept.

I have in my voluminous library a treatise by a famous Cat Mother and expert who tells me that the healthiest cat is the one shut up in a few square yards of a modern block and whose feet never come into contact with either the pavement or a bit of grass. This cat, writes she, is secure from all dangers, contaminations, infections, and is happy. Unfortunately this judgment cannot be accompanied by a testimonial or affidavit signed by a cat. I, for one, cannot agree and my guess would be that the country cat, in spite of the hazards it may encounter, is happier and healthier than the apartment dweller. Certainly it has more fun.

Coop up a cat with yourself in a cliff dwelling and you must come to a decision as to whether or not to alter. Alter! What a word behind which to hide such a despicable deed, and one which must, and in my case does, prey upon the conscience. For it is an arbitrary, brutal, and unilateral tampering with the life and loves of a fellow inhabitant of this earth and so to soften the implication, we do not castrate, we alter, and our household companion becomes a "neuter" and all's well.

But if we do not do so we are also in a fix. Tom, when agitated by the urges of spring, sprays the premises and fills it with an unholy fetor. If confined, his importunings to get out and onto the tiles are hair raising.

Kitty, in heat, and denied a lover raises the roof with deafening plaints of need and desire until you think you will go out of your mind. There is enough sex stimulus about without having your lady cat raucously bringing up the subject. Lulu, one of my Siamese cats, not only yelled the house down but struck attitudes on the rug reminiscent of paintings of famous goddesses or courtesans preparing for a night's work. Venus, Aphrodite, Sappho, and Doll Tearsheet, or Goya's Maja.

Well, there's the problem. If you let the gentleman out, he comes back filthy and bedraggled and perhaps minus an ear left behind in an argument over the lady's favors; if you let the female out unspayed—kittens!

And so, actually, for our own protection and ostensibly to keep our cats "happy" and "contented," we mutilate them.

Now look upon this from the cat's point of view. Here one can only venture into anthropomorphism and consider what our own horror would be like at the prospect, and the rumpus kicked up by proposals for legal sterilization where such might be considered necessary for the public weal.

Whether or not a cat is a thinking, reflective creature, or what our fore-fathers liked to refer to as merely a "dumb animal," there is no doubt but that such creatures have the same sex drives and urges as we and, from the racket that accompanies the ultimate of such a drive, get considerable pleasure out of it. In this we are kin.

Come, will you not admit with me that we have dishonored not only the cat but ourselves and therefore with cat owning comes the carrying about of a considerable amount of guilt?

Now, as to the little matter of tearing things, such as couch covers, brocades on chairs, curtains, tablecloths, drapes, on which cats like to sharpen their claws and exercise the important retractile muscles which enable them to sheath and unsheath these weapons.

What is the alternative? A visit to Hammacher-Schlemmer, Harrods, or Abercrombie and Fitch for the finest hand-crafted scratching post? Your cat will give it one bored tryout and then return to the more pleasurable exercises upon your velvet curtains or silk bedcover. Try to break your cat of these practices and you break your friend as well. Choose!

Now, my feline expert and I part company again for she says cut their claws and both my cat and I feel this dictum monstrous and once more I am faced with problems.

To begin with I would think that my friend is unable to understand my failure to share my soft furnishings. Just because I do not choose to hang from my curtains by my fingernails is no reason why it should not do so and to be scolded or prohibited for a natural act is confusing, bewildering, and upsetting. And as for claw cutting, I consider this a cruel and unusual punishment. If the animal is not wholly confined to a life sentence indoors, the clipped claw is as much of a handicap as if someone were to amputate your toes. It needs them to go up walls or over fences fast, in extremities of pursuit. The claw is not a fingernail to be compared with ours; it is a highly important member of its body and an adjunct to its defense, offense, and mobility. Clip and you stand accused by your cat of unwarranted interference with its person. Don't clip and pay the penalty of ruined counterpanes and upholstery.

Cats get sick. They get awfully sick. Books on how to rear cats list the most appalling illnesses that can befall them which we will not discuss here but which can carry kitty off or lead it to drag itself about the house half-paralyzed, or even infect you. And so you must watch its health as you do that of your child and cheerfully pay the veterinarian's bill. You are familiar with the saying "so-and-so looks like a sick cat," which phrase taken into the language gives us an idea of how pathetic and how heart-rending a sick cat can appear. The damper put upon a household by such a one is almost equal to that of an illness in the family itself. The beast suffers, it cannot speak.

It cannot speak! If it could it would not accuse you of indifference to its plight, but rather of dishonorable negligence which resulted in its getting into such a state for the cat owner goes about his daily business and his own problems, too busy to be aware in time of the symptoms of trouble developing in his pet. One can find any of these in the books devoted to the subject; some are more noticeable than others, a few can be quickly fatal. Through ignorance or carelessness one can lose one's companion overnight or let it slip into a long and lingering malady. The cat has much to complain of here.

And then there is the matter of wanting to go away for a little trip. You wouldn't think twice about taking a dog along with you. Fido goes where you go, but your cat doesn't accompany you for a seaside holiday or a couple of weeks in the mountains skiing.

The peculiar psychology of the cat is partially responsible for this. It doesn't enjoy change and it has registered itself in your mind as being not only independent, but downright disobedient. The dog presents no such problems. It travels in your car (cats get carsick) and it walks to heel, it comes when it's called and is wholly controllable. Imagine trying to take pussy with you to a summer hotel and the complications that would arise.

What then? Leave it with a neighbor? Maybe the neighbor doesn't like animals, maybe the cat doesn't like the neighbor. During your holiday you will never have an easy moment wondering whether kitty has accepted its temporary foster home or has wandered back and is crouched miserably by your front door uncomprehending.

The alternative? The boarding kennels, a two-by-four cage, a wholly bewildering and baffling jail term while you are off enjoying yourself. Unjust to your friend, expensive to you. Your cat has every right to hale you to the bar, accuse you of cruel and unjust punishment, and demand that you be required to spend equal time in the cooler. Cruel and unjust it is, since when you put an animal to board, there is no way that you can communicate to it the fact that this is only a temporary expedient. Your four-footed friend has no sense of time or expiration of sentence. For all it knows it is in for life and may never see you again or return to the comforts of its home. Oh, yes indeed, there is a sad and heinous bill to be drawn up against you.

Consider next all the revolting aspects of the cat box whether it contains sand or mother earth, torn paper, or, at best, that preparation known as "Kitty Litter" and which I am told is now practically universally used throughout the United States and elsewhere and has disinfectant additives.

However, nothing takes away the fact that it is an open affair tucked away in some corner of the apartment, the implications thereof upon which I need not dwell. Not to mention the scattering of particles on the rug or floor when kitty obeys its instincts and attempts to cover its deposits.

Again, what is the alternative? Some member of the household is delegated to take it out.

But taking puss out in no way resembles taking Fido out. The dog, being a dog, is immediately, compulsively and happily attracted to residues of the products of other dogs. Three sniffs, a couple of inspections, the decision as to the most recent and attractive one and the job is done.

Not so cat. You can spend a frustrated hour while it thinks it over. It may or may not know why you have brought it down; it may or may not have the urge, but the point is, it doesn't care. What it considers really wonderful is that it is free and there are all sorts of things and places to be investigated or climbed. In short, it's a kind of holiday. The so fervently desired elimination becomes only incidental and at the cat's own pleasure. Or, it suddenly decides to play the "Whee-you-can't-catch-me" game in which for a frustrating two hours it keeps just out of reach. Or, if for a moment you relax your vigilance, it simply disappears.

Whichever way you look at it, this function when confined to a room or set of rooms is a nuisance and the cat is just as uncomfortable and unhappy about it as you are, and compelled to behave in a way that is wholly unnatural to it. Oh, I know that it can be trained to worship at the altar of our great God Loo, but spare me your photographs of kitty perched upon the rim of the porcelain well "doing its business," for I cannot bear the sight, and when they are sent to me by proud cat owners, I invariably drop them into my wastebasket, for this is a mockery of everything that is cat.

What are some of the other handicaps of ownership? Cat hairs all over the place, ostracism by phobe friends, priceless or sentimental articles knocked off the mantel as a result of one of those sudden, lunatic, flying journeys around the joint, not to mention the fact that just as we have made ourselves comfortable we become aware that the cat is on the wrong side of the door.

The cat has a longer list of attainder including being given as a toy before a child is old enough to understand relationships to animals or has been taught the difference between play and injury.

The least honorable of us abandon cats, leave them in empty houses when we move away, throw them out of cars in the country, or turn them loose in the cities to starve.

Well, the examination is concluded and if it has shown that cat owning is indeed a not unmixed blessing, it would also seem to indicate that the greater debt is on our side and the cat has far more of which to complain. I, for one, am grateful that it forgives the outrages perpetrated upon it and generously consents to continue to live with me.

Love

I have one final problem I would like to discuss with you. I sometimes wish I knew what my cat thinks of or feels for me. Or do I? And do you ever, and ought we perhaps to leave well enough alone and not pry?

I have loved my cats with a curious kind of affection unlike that of any other emotion that I have experienced for man or beast and one which I have never, up to this point, tried to analyze, dissect, or understand. And now that I try to do so I think that it is compounded of admiration, sympathy, and amusement. To this I add a slight and curious tincture of pity plus a wholly unpredictable and irrational feeling which comes welling up out of depths indefinable.

Somewhere, sometime, this extraordinary thing happened between humans and felines.

Looking backward, our original association was simply mutually and practically rewarding and wholly unsentimental. When first man learned to store his grain he found that mice got into it. The cat was a hunter and small rodents his natural prey. Clever man therefore engaged a cat to help him save his food by putting it where it could hunt to its heart's content and serve man by doing so.

We know that this situation obtained in Egypt so long ago because this is the first record in painting and writing that we have of this relationship. It is most curious. Primitive man was beginning to save up food long before the Pharaohs. Dog helped him to hunt, but there is no record of cat assisting him to store.

On the banks of the Nile then, where originally was established this perfect mutual arrangement and balance, one day or one millennium something inexplicable happened; the ferocious guardian of the granaries became a cold, distant, high-placed and worshipped god in the temples.

The cat in those times was even further involved with humans in that it performed the service eventually usurped by the bird dog and accompanied its owner on the hunt as testified by wall paintings showing a definitely striped tabby lurking in the reeds of the swamps to put up a bird. And not only that but the animal was further willing to act as retriever after the hunter had brought down the quarry with an arrow, spear, or throwing-stick. It didn't take it too long to discover it was being conned.

All in all, for an animal which up to that time appeared not to have been heard of, or noticed, it accomplished the neatest trick of the ages of which the most astonishing and enduring was the manner in which it crept into the hearts and minds of men, women, and children and established itself in the home, and there inspired not only awe, worship, and respect, but above everything else that mattered—love. The paintings and the written records show that the ancient Egyptians pampered and spoiled their house cats, treated them as honored guests, and loved them. But did the cats love the Egyptians, and when and how did that love come about in the breast of that feral creature, or wherever the seat of that emotion might be, and does my cat love me?

I raise the question, because whereas it is easy for those of us so constituted to be drawn toward those soft, beautiful, and admirable animals, if I were of their species, I think I would find man very difficult to love.

In fact, taking my cat's point of view, it ought to regard me as something of an unstable and capricious lunatic, stupid, unpredictable, tyrannical, and utterly selfish; satisfactory for board and lodging and an occasional caress, but for the rest utterly useless.

Well, admitted that uselessness is no bar to affection as many men have discovered, what, besides food and shelter, have I to offer to my four-footed companion except that human type of possessive love that even humans eventually find cloying and my cat certainly does.

By and large they will take just so much of it. When we love members of our own species we take them in our arms and press them to our hearts. Cats don't like to be squeezed. For that matter they do not care for any manner of confinement and will only rest quiescent in one's grasp for a period they consider polite before starting a scramble for the floor.

They will take only so much petting, tickling, rubbing, or mauling before, smothering a yawn, they will walk away with a firmness that is unmistakable. And if still you fail to get the message, they will either leave the room entirely, or produce a toy from where it has been stashed beneath the bureau and start a game.

A gentleman cat who loves a lady cat embraces her right enough in what is a combination of a football charge and an all-in wrestling match at the climax of which the object of his amour gets a severe bite in her neck. But we are not considering that kind of love. And besides, when our cat does give it to us, that is to say, when in play we sometimes unwittingly stimulate it sexually and it digs the claws of all four feet into our arm and gives our hand a nip as well, we yell blue murder and accuse the animal of being false, sly, and treacherous.

It is a human fallacy, the belief that love must engender love and the like, in intensity, to that bestowed. This illusion has been getting men into trouble with women and themselves ever since the emotion was discovered and classified. "But I love you so," pleads the unhappy and idiot swain. "How can you possibly not love me in return?" And even when there exists a mutuality of affection, people lovers want to make it quantitative. "Do you love me as much as I love you?" They wish to put it onto a scale and see whether it balances or which way it tips. We at least can find out linguistically or lie decently to one another. But my wise, dumb animal isn't saying.

And so I wonder whether it has the mechanism of love, the kind of which I am thinking; unphysical, abstract, yet deeply felt, surging and impelling, the kind which is not "made" but which simply happens when the object thereof comes within range.

For there is always the lurking suspicion in all of us of the power of the cupboard. Was there in bygone days a real cat deity, a supercat who one moment, smitten with a stroke of genius, discovered and imparted to all that followed it that man is the eternal sucker who can be flattered or conned into anything with the right approach? When ofttimes we are compelled to the same doubts as to the sincerity of the fervent declarations of undying passion from members of our own kind, what is so strange in suspecting that our cat maybe is putting on the act of the ages?

In fact, one would have to be wholly besotted with one's own worth *not* to wonder, knowing the cat's reserve and independence. Suspicion is further an outgrowth of the fact that they can turn it on and they can turn it off. And if, for the most part you seem to remember that they turn it on when there would appear to be something in it for them, then you suddenly remember that day when you sat depressed in a chair, suffering from a hurt concealed, a worry, a disappointment, or a crisis, and suddenly there was someone soft and furry in your lap and a body pressed close to yours in warmth and comfort.

Or there is the presentation mouse which would come wrapped in white tissue and tied with a golden ribbon if a cat could. Or the waiting by the gate or door for you to come home or some other strange mark of unselfish feeling. Everyone who has ever kept a cat has a story to tell in proof.

I wrote earlier of the element of pity that was a part of the emotion I feel and sometimes I wonder whether it is not upon this level that mutuality is established and that my wise and well-adjusted cat is feeling sorry for me and would like to help me to be more like its quiet and contented self.

The true animal lover will understand my use of the word pity, not in the sense of patronizing, for in that there is nothing akin to love, but rather a sympathy with and for them, for their lot, which is not an easy one anymore than is ours. It will be then just as easy to love a hippopotamus as much as a prize Persian, or a jackal, dingo, or hyena as much as a Seal Point Siamese or a silver tabby. More so, perhaps, since the former haven't got it so good and need it so much more.

No, this compassion, I think, stems from the fact that in one way or another, we are all in the same trap of life cycle and in the short time allotted us are trying to make out the best we can. And the cat more often than not has a hard row to hoe.

This creature is also the least insistent upon pity which in itself is attractive and breeds the respect that is often the backbone of love. While it is constantly demanding the best, we have seen that it will also do without. The cat can be spoiled rotten, but basically life has taught it to expect little. It is a master of survival on its own terms. It may be an expert at panhandling you or tugging at your heart, but it is always to be remembered that essentially it promises nothing in return, and then suddenly, at the most surprising and unexpected of moments, gives freely.

Well, there you are, and as the saying goes, we have come a "fur piece" from the beginning of the journey without getting any forrader. One starts out by reflecting upon one's house pet and winds up with a self-analysis that is not too flattering with genuine communication reduced to a few signals affording only rare and actually reliable glimpses into the mind and heart of one's cat. And if out of this one is able to salvage something at least slightly admirable in oneself as voluntary associates of this creature, it is the fact that one, in some measure, is able to bear to love something or someone without expecting a return.

Odes to Honorable Cat

HONORABLE CAT

I am Cat.
I am honorable.
I have pride.
I have dignity.
And I have memory.
For I am older than you.
I am older than your Gods; the Tree Gods, the Stone Gods,
The Thunder and Lightning and the Sun Gods
And your God of Love.
I too can love
But with only half a heart
And that I offer you.
Accept what I am able to give
For were I to give you all
I could not bear your inevitable treachery.
Let us remain honorable friends.

BUTTERFLIES WERE MADE

TO PLAY WITH

Butterflies were made for us to play with.
They do not know where they are going,
And we have to guess.
That's what makes it exciting.
If Butterflies were not so silly
It would be easy.
Once we caught three Butterflies in an afternoon
But afterwards we were sorry.
They couldn't fly anymore.
They just lay in the grass
And sighed sadly with their wings.
That was no fun.

THE CHAIR

This is my chair.
Go away and sit somewhere else.
This one is all my own.
It is the only thing in your house that I possess,
And insist upon possessing.
Everything else therein is yours.
My dish,
My toys,
My basket,
My scratching post and my Ping-Pong ball;
You provided them for me.
This chair I selected for myself.
I like it,
It suits me.
You have the sofa,
The stuffed chair
And the footstool.
I don't go and sit on them do I?
Then why cannot you leave me mine,
And let us have no further argument?

ERROR

The flowers think they are more beautiful than we,
But they are wrong.

MISERY'S FENCE

There is a hole in Misery's fence.
They cannot shut you in
And they cannot shut you out
When you are nothing,
Or nobody;
Lost,
Sick,
Sore,
Or hungry;
Frightened, homeless, hopeless,
It doesn't really matter
Which side you're on
Does it?

SPEECH

When I have things to say
I expect you to listen to me.
If you cannot understand what I am saying
That is your fault and your loss,
But at least be quiet when I am speaking
And try to comprehend
You who think yourselves so clever,
Who know languages of the people
Of the living world and the dead,
Why cannot you learn mine
Which is so simple
To express wants so few?
"In"
"Out"
"Hungry"
"Thirsty"
"Give me just a taste of what you are having."
"Something hurts."
"My ball has rolled under the divan; get it out."
"Stop doing whatever it is you are doing and pay more attention to me."
"I like you."
"I don't like you."
If you can talk to the Arabs, the Chinese, the Eskimos
And read the hieroglyphics of the past, why cannot you understand me?
Try!

SPYING

Very well,
So you've caught me going out.
What is it that is worrying you?
That I might be going to meet a lady friend?
Catch a bird?
Frighten a dog?
Steal someone's roast off the kitchen table?
Get dirty?
I might.
So what?
Why don't you let me live my own life
As I let you live yours?
Do I bother about where you are going,
Or what you will get up to
When you leave the house?
You might be going off to visit your neighbor's wife,
You could be going to hurt a friend,
Or cheat somebody in business,
Or tell a lie,
Or steal,
Or in your own way come home, dirty.
But it's none of my affair.
So would you kindly keep your nose out of mine.

RENDEZVOUS

I am waiting for my mistress to come home from school.
She is nine years old,
Accounted by us as still a kitten.
She is gone from early morn
Until the sun is low.
I miss her.
When she is in the house
My purr throbs in my throat.
When she is gone
I go to her empty room
And lie on something
That is hers,
And wait until I know
She will be coming down the street,
Carrying her satchel,
Her braids swinging as she skips.
Sometimes when she walks with friends
She will ignore me and forget
That I am there.
I will come down from where I perch
And follow her,
My tail her banner,
My song of joy her music,
For all that matters is
That she is home again.
Or she will pluck me from the wall
And hold me to her lips and talk to me
And I could die of love.
She plays with me as though I were a toy,
Clothed in doll's dresses,
Or perched in the high chair
That once was hers.

She lifts me by tender legs,
Holds me to her across my middle,
Or wears me like a shawl across her shoulders;
Cradles me in her arms
Pretending I am her kitten,

And sings me lullabies.
I know her smells,
Her hair, her apron and her ribbons,
The orange and the sticky sweet she had for lunch
Still on her fingers and her clothes.
Her shrill voice sometimes hurts my ears;
Her careless feet have often trod my tail;
Her scoldings and her storms of anger
I endure.
But when she weeps I leap into her lap
To try to comfort her.
I lick the salt tears from her face,
Feel her damp cheek press into my fur
And share her misery,
Until once more her laughter comes.
She doesn't laugh, she gurgles with delight,
A sound mysterious as my purr
And she will snatch me up
And hug me fiercely so that I must cry out.
Her voice then tells me she is sorry,
And we are friends.

I have no register for Time,
Moonrise and sunrise only.
I cannot count the passage of the days,
Or solve the mysteries of clocks,
Minutes and seconds
A beginning or an end.
And yet, each day within me
There strikes the hour of her return.
I know,
And I am here to meet her.

STATEMENT

A blossom bright has caught my eye.
I mean to have it down. For I
Am ME and me is all
That counts upon this spinning ball.

THE COMMUNAL DISH

If you must really know
The cause of my contempt and anger,
Need you look further
Than the indignity you put upon us;
This communal dish?
Are you then so poor
You cannot give us each his bowl
From which to eat
In privacy?
Are you so thoughtless that you cannot see
How we are shamed
By thrusting nose to nose
Like pigs
Crowding to gain our sustenance
At the trough?
Have we who once were gods then sunk so low?
Or is it you?
The blood of Bast flows in my veins
And in my temple I was ritually fed.
My dish was carved of Lapis Lazuli,
Carnelian, Chrysophase, Agate, or Onyx,
Or Chalcedony.
Necklaces of Turquoise, Amethyst, and Opal
Adorned my throat,
And beads of amber.
The moonstone glistened from my forehead.
In my temple carved from
Blood-red granite stone,
Priestesses carried me my food
And retired lest they blaspheme
By lessening my majesty.
The music of flutes mingled with the soft whisper
Of the sistrum.
In solitude sublime
I ate.

Dignity, dignity, dignity.
They bestowed dignity upon us.
Time has robbed us of our godhead,
But our dignity never.
Where we are more than one, then,
I beg of you, leave us this memory
Of vanished luster.
We do not ask for plates of Royal Crown,
Wedgwood, Worcester, Sevres, or Dresden,
Gold-edged or patterned with design
Like yours.
A simple receptacle of earth or wood or iron,
Is all we ask, but each to his own
To dine
In seemly decency.

OH HOW DIFFICULT IT IS

TO BE YOUNG

Oh how difficult it is to be young
And worried.
Like me.
I worry all the time.
What will it be like when I am grown?
What will become of me?
Where will I live, and with whom?
Will I have a home?
Will I be loved?
Will I be rich?
Or must I work?
Will I travel and see the world?
Or spend my life in one room in a basket?
Who will have me and what will THEY be like?
Or must I roam the alleyways
For fish heads
And shiver through the nights of sleet and rain
Behind some billboard?
What will life be like?
I who know nothing
But one long worry
Find it very difficult to be young.

I SHOULD HAVE BROUGHT

MY CAN OPENER

Good creatures, you have me at a loss
With your aggressive attitude
Toward one who harbors no ill will,
Nor ill intent.
For though I seem to lick my lips in contemplation
The gesture's purely retrospect
Of how I do remember you at home,
As sweet white meat immured in cans
Opened and placed as treat upon my plate
Unmenacing.

You see me for departure poised?
'Tis just that pressing business calls me elsewhere
And not your warlike gestures,
Your crusted armor,
The threatening clapper of your shears
The reinforcement at your side
The dry rustle of impenetrable shells.
And thus I think we each might backward turn
Upon his own respective ways,
Each to his element.
Oil, cats, and water do not mix
Nor cats with crayfish mingle.
Except where you are labeled
"Packed in Japan" and "For Export Only."
And so I say you, "Peace."
And too, "Farewell."

JEWELRY

If you but could
You would pluck out my eyes
And wear them set in rings on your fingers
Or ornaments in your ears
My so-called friend
And animal lover.

THE DOOR

You and your doors
Shut the door!
Open the door!
Have you locked the door?
See who's at the door,
Who left the door open?
Where's the doorman?
Knock at the door.
Doors, doors, doors,
Who needs them?
They tell us you invented them to keep people out
And still haven't tumbled
To the fact
That by doing so
You are shutting yourselves in.
We can work a swing door
See fig. 1
And then see fig. 2
Dangerous!
We could get our paws crushed,
Or have our tails pinched.
Doors,
And your eternal complaints
That we are always on the wrong side.
Who is?
You are, not we.
You want us out when we're in and in when we're out.
You and your door psychology.
Front door,
Back door,
Side door,
Veranda door,
Bedroom door,
Kitchen door,
Cupboard door,
Study door.

And to have to listen to you!
"Oh for God's sakes, the cat wants to go out again.
Somebody let her."
Or "Is that damned cat out again?

Open the door and let her in
Or she'll shout the house down."
On the other hand it's pretty funny.
Do you know what you've managed to make of yourselves?
A bunch of doormen for us cats.

BIRDS

I would not dignify a bird by chasing it,
Or demean myself by flying.
I could fly if I wished to.
I do not wish to fly
Besides, flying is unfair.

PRIDE

I am a champion,
And win prizes at exhibitions.
In my opinion I am the best damn cat
In the whole show.
And any judge who doesn't agree is blind.
Look at me,
I am perfect.
Arrogance?
Not at all.
Self-knowledge
No false modesty here.
I know your pious quotation,
"Pride goeth before a fall."
How very middle class.
Where pride is based on such a one as me
There can be no fall.
So don't waste your time waiting around for it.

ALWAYS PAUSE ON THE THRESHOLD

The wise cat pauses on the threshold
Before emerging from the house.
I fan my whiskers like antennae
To pluck the signals of lurking danger
From the air
I know them all:
Dogs, boys, boots, wheels, hoofs, and unfriendly cats,
Sticks that beat, stones that fly, feet that kick.
All these generate hostility
Of the perilous streets
That taint the air.
The city jungle's pungencies
I sample with my sensors
Before I venture forth
Forewarned.

THE DANDELION

I am smelling a dandelion.
I smell it because I like it.
People say dandelions don't smell good.
I say they do.
Come, smell a dandelion with me.

THE WIZARD

Dog, beware!
For I am a great wizard
Who has turned himself into a beast
One hundred cubits tall,
With jaws that gape,
And teeth more fearful than the fangs
Of ancient dragons.
My claws are like the scythes
That armed the wheels of warrior chariots.
My eyes flash fire,
I exhale poisonous smoke,
And could devour you at a bite.
Dog, if you are wise you will agree.
Do not account me
A small and timid creature
Arching its back to try to frighten you.
Just go away and do not compel me
To break my spell
And retire up a tree.

JUDGMENT

O thou great omnipotent, two-legged God of mine
Upon whose brow lieth all wisdom,
Whose eye pierceth the darkness
And bringeth light,
Who sits in the High Place,
And judgeth right from wrong,
And good from evil,
And the straight from the crooked path
And the saved from the damned,
From whom nothing is hidden,
Ai! Thou knowest I have been into the cream jug.
What wilt thou do to me?

TETHER

Let me go, you blind, heartless and unutterable fool,
For you have lost my love
And cannot keep me
At a leash's end
Like a stinking dog.
Let me go!
Let me go!
Let me go!
Ere my heart breaks.
For I am cat
And you cannot bind me
As you have tethered your every other love
To its destruction.
What more could you desire
Than that I sat upon your knee
And gave you company?
What else could you demand
Than that I was content to curl before the fireside
And lend your house the blessing of my presence?
And so because you are a weakling,
You have tied me to your failures.
All I would have had you be,
And now I know that you are not,
Has parted us forever.
For you have robbed me of my dignity,
And I can love you nevermore.

"AND LEAD US NOT INTO . . ."

Good friends,
Spare us your indignation,
And all that self-righteous anger.
What do you expect of us?
To be ascetics?
Just keep the dining room door shut
And there won't be any problems.

MORNING

The morning sun
Banishes the shadows
Back to their dark corners.
See how it stalks them
Across the meadow
And kindles every leaf
To light my day.

CAMOUFLAGE

Have you ever in your life
Felt you wanted
Or needed
To be invisible?
Well then,
This,
Is how it is done.

COUNTER
CAMOUFLAGE

On the other hand,
If you'd like people
  to notice you,
And most of the time
We *want* to be noticed,
It's simply a matter
Of choosing
The proper background.

I LURK

I lurk,
I am in hiding,
No one must know that I am here.
I have my reasons.
I see but I am not seen.
An old man passes, his shoulders bowed with memories,
I will not add one more to his burden.
A boy rides by on a bicycle,
How clever he is.
A little girl drags her doll behind her.
I will not jump out at the doll.
It would not hurt the toy;
The little girl might never forget.
Here is a wise man, a teacher.
He walks in knowledge.
He knows what makes a clock strike,
The sun turn red,
Fire burn,
Winds blow,
Rain fall,
And the earth shake,
But he does not know that I am here.
I see a rich man roll by in his glass prison,
Everyone can see him;
Everyone knows that he is there.
I am secret and unseen.
There goes a poor man dressed in rags
His worn shoes whisper by.
I could make him richer by revealing myself.
I will not do so,
His poverty is dear to him.
I lurk, I hide, I watch.
No one knows I am here.
I know.

CONFESSION

I've been named Poosie, and
I am spoiled
Thoroughly, thoroughly spoiled, and I like it.
And don't let anyone tell you different.
I lie upon the softest cushions,
Under the downiest covers
And love every moment.
I get the cream off the top of the milk every day
And special double thick, heavy on Sundays,
And I lap it up.
My owner is besotted.
She hugs and kisses me
And carries me around with her all day,
And talks to me
And I enjoy it.
I'm spoiled rotten, and, friends,
That's the life.
Whatever I want, I cry for,
Crab, lobster, caviar, fish roes, sardines, filet, white meat of chicken,
You name it,
She's got it,
I get it.
I don't want to work, or hunt.
If ten snow-white mice were to saunter past my nose,
I wouldn't lift a paw.
I'm greedy, graceless, shameless, lazy,
And luxury loving.
Everything that comes my way I take,
And yell for more.
I'm spoiled useless.
I admit it.
And I adore it.

SHORT POEM DESCRIPTIVE OF SOMEONE
IN A HURRY WITH SOME-
THING IMPORTANT
ON HIS
MIND

Gangway!

GOOD NEWS

Good morning.
There's Good News, brethren,
Yea, Good News.
I am the Devil,
Yea, His Majesty Himself.
I have chosen to present myself to you in this form,
From which I trust you will recoil,
Since the face of evil
Is sufficient unto your innocence,
To mark me.
For I am Satan,
Lucifer,
Prince of Darkness,
Tempter,
Adversary,
Anti-Christ,
Diabolus,
Shaitan,
Eblis,
Apollyon,
The Evil One
And Ahriman.
I am also known for purposes of identification as Mephistopheles,
His Satanic Majesty,
The Old Gentleman,
Old Nick,
Old Harry,
Old Scratch,
Old Gooseberry,
Old Horny
And Old Clootie.
You may also have heard of me under the name of Asmodeus,
Azazeel,
Belial,
And Beelzebub.
Very well then, I am the Devil Himself
And I bring you a message of good cheer.

And the Word I have for you
Is that it is I and not God who really rules the universe.
Hallelujah to me!
Hosannah to Hell!
Te Deum to the Fiend!
And behold how easily all that has been worrying you
Falls into place.
You need no longer be bewildered
By the paradox of your loving God.
It is I, not He who has sent you wars,
Fire,
Flood,

Disasters,
Starvation,
Genocide,
The mass slaughter of the Innocents,
And the killing and maiming of little children.
I have endowed you with greed,
Mistrust,
Envy,
Jealousy,
Hatred and lust.
I have dirtied your mind,
Led you to pollute the air you breathe,
And the lands and the waters,
And I have hung the concept and the passion for money like a millstone
    'round your necks.
No loving God would bring you to such a pass.
It is Me you must placate
And flatter.
It is Me you must beseech, pray, sing and dance to.
It is My name you must take in vain, cry out,
"The Devil help me!"
And "Oh my Devil!"
And "The Devil be with you,"
For it is I who have made you
What you have become today
Unfit for Paradise
And not too welcome either
Below.
Look upon Me and acknowledge that it is I
Who have been the power
Since the beginning of Time.
God is a minor poet
Who once long ago
Wrote some verse about love
Which you have never quite managed to understand.

QUERY

Little striped chipmunk,
Why do you hang upside down?
Or is it you
Who are right side up,
And I who am standing on my head?

THE SECRET

Oh . . .
I didn't know you were there.
I have just come from a secret place
Where I have had a secret thought.
The secret thought
Was beautiful.
The secret place somewhere
Where you will never find it.
Sometimes I can't even find it
Myself.
I wish I could tell you
My secret thought
It was so beautiful
Or where I thought of it
But then it wouldn't be secret anymore
For you'd know.

THE PLAINT OF THE CALICO CAT

If you can put together
Flowers of any color,
Pink with red,
Red with orange,
Orange with brown,
Brown with black,
Black with yellow,
Yellow with white
And people think they are beautiful,
Why should I who am some of all these colors
Be considered ugly?

THE BALLAD OF TOUGH TOM

That's right!
Those are tufts of my fur you're looking at.
What about it?
You don't see the other cat, do you?
What are a few hairs
Compared to an ear?
I didn't get the whole of his off
Because by then he was already heading south,
Having had enough.
But it was eminently satisfactory.
My name is Tough Tom,
And I am King of the Car Park.
When the sun shines
It warms the hoods of the cars for us.
We like that.
We lie on them.
Sometimes we get chased because
We leave footmarks on the cars,
But most of the time nobody bothers,
We have our own crowd that comes here
To sun.
But I say who does and who doesn't.
See?
Because I'm King of the Car Park.
So one day this stranger walks up and says,
"What's your name?"
So I says, "Tough Tom
And I'm King of the Car Park. What's yours?"
And he says, "Tough Charlie, and I guess
You ain't King of the Car Park anymore."
"Oh, I get it," I says, "You're looking for a little action."
"How did you guess?" says Tough Charlie.
I'm measuring him up in the meantime
And he's a lot of cat.

Yellow and white.
Yellow is a color I ain't partial to.
And although I wasn't looking for trouble that morning,
Like now my being King of the Car Park,
It was up to me to oblige. So I says,
"Shall we dispense with the preliminaries?
See now, like the growling
And the fluffing

And the humping up
And the exchange of insults?"
Waste of time
When you know you're going to mix.
"Okay by me," says Tough Charlie, "Let's go!"
And he's up and onto me, leading with his right.
Oh boy, a sucker punch.
But I guess I'm a little dopey,
Lying out in that hot sun,
On that warm hood
And maybe he's got a half a pound on me as well.
So I'm on my back before I know it,
And he just misses getting my eye out.
Tough Charlie he was all right.
I give my left on the end of his nose
And try a roll-over
But he's too smart for that
And goes for my eye again, only this time
I'm waiting for it.
He don't get the eye,
But I get his ear.
Brother!
We're all over that car,
Down on the ground,
And underneath,
And back up on top again,
With the gang sitting around
Waiting to see
Who is the King of the Car Park.
He gives me the raking kick
With the back legs.
That's when I lost all that fur
You see about.
But I've still got that ear,
And it's starting to come away.
Tough Tom and Tough Charlie
And the battle of the Car Park!
They'll sing about that one on the tiles
For many a night.

So I guess maybe Tough Charlie thinks it over,
That with only one ear
He ain't gonna do so good anymore
With the broads, and he says,
"Okay, so I was wrong. Leggo!
You're still King of the Car Park."
So I had to laugh, and he's off
With what's left of his ear.
That's the story.
So now for a little clean-up.
I'm still Tough Tom,
King of the Car Park.

DIALOGUE

"Japanese goldfish,
With your gossamer tail,
You are the loveliest creature
I have ever seen."

"Japanese kitten,
Put your tongue back in where it belongs
And go away.
I know exactly what you are thinking."

SLEEP

Cat's cradle,
Cat's slumber,
Soft slumber;
Sleep softly
All cats.

I am a well-read cat.
I quote:
"Sleep that knits up
The ruffled fur
By thoughtless human hands
Disturbed." [1]
"Yet a little sleep,
A little slumber,
A crossing of the paws,
To sleep." [2]
"Above my deep
And dreamless sleep,
The stealthy mice
Creep by." [3]
"See how I enjoy
The honeyheavy dew
Of slumber.
No phantasies or figures
Of blows, kicks or pursuit,
Therefore I do sleep sound." [4]
"Oh sweet are the slumbers
Of the virtuous cat." [5]
"Hark to the word of old Ginge:
It is well to hunt and keep
Mousehole vigil,
But better than all
Is to sleep, sleep, sleep.
There's nothing, nothing, nothing,
I say,
That's worth the lying awake." [6]
"For who can wrestle against sleep?" [7]
"Good night, good night,
I shall say good night,

'Til it be tomorrow:
A thousand times good night." [8]
Now it's me again.

        Drowsy, drowsy,
        Dozing away the futile hours,
        What wouldn't you give to be a cat
        Instead of what you are?

[1] Shakespeare: *Macbeth,* Act II, Sc. 1.
[2] Proverbs: 1.6.
[3] Phillips Brooks: "O Little Town of Bethlehem."
[4] The Bard of Avon again: *Julius Caesar,* Act II, Sc. 1.
[5] Joseph Addison: *Cato,* Act V, Sc. 1.
[6] Agnes Lee: "Motherhood," Stanzas 1 & 3.
[7] Martin Tupper: "Of Beauty."
[8] Shakespeare, my favorite: *Romeo and Juliet,* Act II, Sc. 2.

U.F.O.

All hail, thou Unidentified Flying Object
From what fathomless distances art thou come?
From whence and where and when
Didst thou escape gravity's embrace
And quit the starlit caverns of eternity
To span the corridors of timelessness
And bridge a thousand light years
To come to me?
Oh thou brave visitor
From outer space
Daring the Cosmos
On the wings of stellar winds,
Impenetrable night and deadly dust
And silences.
Silences frozen until their crackling roar
Shattered the emptiness.
Didst thou greet the nebulae?
What are the quasars and the pulsars like?
Were there great monsters on the way?
Was Andromeda as fair as Perseus spoke?
Didst draw Orion's sword
Against the menace of The Bear?
Descend, descend, thy journey's at an end.
Read me the riddle of Infinity,
Tell me the story that never ends.

Whoever sent thee to me,
Thou art welcome,
Oh thou wondrous Object,
Thou . . .
Why, why . . .
Thou . . . I mean *you* art nothing but an old empty red paper bag
And not from outer space at all.
I'll have a little look inside.
Just as I thought.
Well, we can all make mistakes, can't we?
Pity about all that poetry I've wasted . . .

106

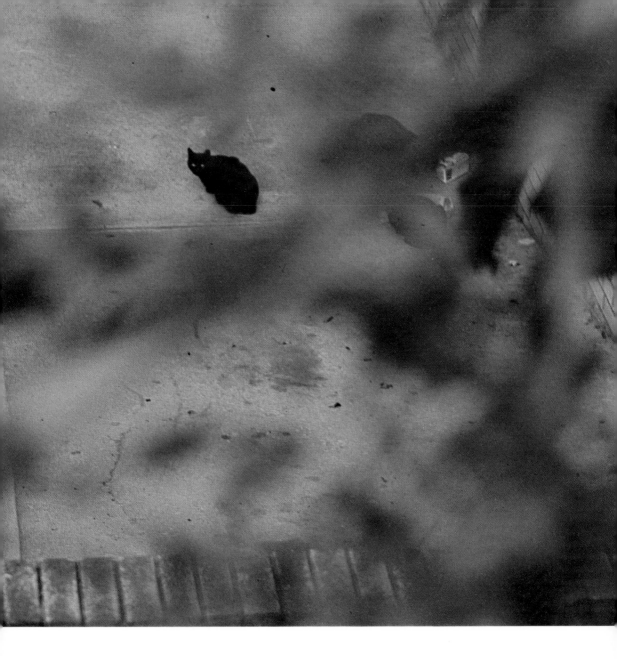

NIGHT WATCHER

The hurtful day
Leaves its imprint on the night,
And dreams
That pierce the walls of dwellings
Silent in slumber.
I keep the watches of the night,
Sentinel to man's nocturnal guilt.

Ghosts of his memories,
Borne on the wings of manic laughter,
Anger, regret, and tears
Cry about me.
They cannot touch my innocence.
Keeping lone vigil here
'Til the stars pale;
They pass me by.

CHOCOLATE BOX

We are the Chocolate Box Kittens!
Sweet, sweet, sweet!
"Oh the little darlings
We could just eat you!"
Yes, eat us, eat us, eat us!
Nougat, caramels, marshmallow,
Chocolate liqueur, chocolate cherries, chocolate-covered nuts,
Turkish delight, crystallized fruits, peppermint creams,
Peanut brittle, toffee sticks, marzipan.
"Oh the dears, so cuddly and soft!"
Yes, soft, soft, soft,
Soft centers, mocha cream, strawberry, pistachio,
Raspberry, lemon flavor, bonbons, pralines, and truffles.
Soft centers, hard centers, Brazil nuts and walnuts, peanuts and almonds,
Coconut, ginger root, filberts and hazelnuts.
Sweet, sweet, sweet.
Eat us, take some, have one.
Butterscotch, anise drops, liquorice,
Milk chocolate, sweet chocolate, bitter chocolate,
Candied violets, maraschino, sugarplums, orange creams,
Coffee, mocha, brandy centers.
Sweet, sweet, eat, eat!
"O dear, I think we are going to be sick!"

SILENCE

I walk on secret feet,
Though if I willed,
My tread
Would shake the earth beneath me.
I stalk
As silently as moonrise,
The sinking of a leaf,
The touch of snow upon the ground.
A drop of dew, born to a petal,
The frost spreading upon a windowpane,
The shadow of a cloud
Drifting,
Make no more sound than I.
Nor with my hunting
Do I stir a fallen leaf.
I come,
I go,
Unheard by day,
Unseen by night,
On muffled feet of steel
Clad in velvet shoes.

TIGER?

Tiger, tiger burning bright,
Blazing headlamps in the night
Some immortal hand or brain
Has taught me to keep out of rain.

When the storm clouds shroud the stars,
I take shelter under cars,
When they go, the passing showers,
I come forth to smell the flowers.

With the tears from Heaven rent,
Blossoms synthesize their scent.
He who smiles this work to see
Also smiles since He made me.
Tiger, tiger burning bright
Shining orbs that pierce the night,
What immortal hand did make
Me and also William Blake?

SET PIECE

I'm a porcelain cat *
On a bamboo mat,
And that's that.

* Not really.

JOURNEY TO NOWHERE

I simply don't know where I am going
Or why,
Or what it was I started out to do.
Haven't you ever felt like this?
You had something in your head,
Something you wanted to accomplish,
Or some place you wanted to go,
And halfway there you've forgotten what it was
Or where
Or even, for that matter, why.
I know I started out on a most important errand
And now suddenly I can't remember
Where it is I am going
Or why
Or what for.

STANDOFF

I have traveled considerably,
But I must say
That never before have I encountered
Anything as curious as you.
Packing your house upon your back
Or pretending to be a tank.
Turtle, I believe you are called
Member of the aquatic Chelonia,
Which is quite a mouthful.
Well I am known as Felis catus
Which isn't bad either.
Nevertheless, and however,
Considered from both the professional
And aesthetic standpoint,
I don't dig you.
They say you are edible.
I've never had any.
Your armor plating I consider
Manifestly unfair
And I should say your attitude
Leaves me in doubt
As to the wisdom
Of closer examination.
Shall we both think this over a little further,
And not be precipitate?

THE HAUNTED RUG

Do you believe in ghosts?
I do,
Because I am one.
Regulation,
And of course white.
Just you wait.
You'll see
I'm haunting a rug.
It's frightening when I move
Isn't it?
Are you terrified?
Mystified?
Goggle-eyed?
Tongue-tied?
And shall we say
Petrified?
Actually fossilized?
Splendid!

That's my idea of a successful haunt.
All right then
I'll come out,
But first I have to say a spell.
Ready?
Hocus-pocus Rumpelstiltskin,
Meshach, Shadrach, and 'Bednego,
Ibbity, bibbity, sibbity saab,
Congo, bongo, piscator!
Help!
I'm caught!
I can't get out!
Quick, do you know any more magic words?
Eeny, meeny, miney mo,
Megantic Ypsilanti Pusillanimous,
Okeechobee Pumpkin Pie,
Cascara Mascara O'Hara Spelunk,
Tintinnabulation, one, two, three, parabaloo!
Hey Johnny-jump-up, where are you?
Higgledy-piggledy coruscate,
Equate,

Oblate,
Marinate,
Federate,
Absquatulate,
Episcopate,
Prestidigitate!
Phew! That worked!
Here I am.
I can't bear to be confined.
Now, what was it I was saying.
Oh yes, I'm a ghost.
Boo!

THE MYSTERY

I cannot think why there should be
Two instead of one of me.
I am furry, round, and fat,
The other one is thin and flat.
I do not understand at all,
Why I'm both here and on the wall.
'Tis so as plainly you can see.
Can you explain this mystery?

THE INSULT

I have been insulted.
My feelings have been hurt
And I am not coming back into the house.
You laughed at me.
Don't think that I was fooled.
You weren't laughing *with* me
But AT me
When I lost my balance
Washing,
And fell over.
You laughed,
And it wasn't funny.
All my grace, control, and dignity were gone;
You robbed me of my image of myself
And with your braying
All but destroyed my pride.
Don't think I cannot take a joke.
There's nothing lacking with my sense of humor,
I just don't like being made to look ridiculous.
It's no use your standing there calling,
"Kitty, kitty, kitty!"
Or offering me bribes.
Your coarse laughter
Has offended me deeply
And it may take me some time to get over it,
Or never.
If and when I come back at all
It will be
In my own sweet time.

TRIO

Jiggarum, Juggarum, Purrrrrrrr Miaow
Two frogs on a stump,
One cat on a stump,

"What is the meaning of life, my friends?
"Who thought it up?
"What is the sense of it?
"What is the end?
"That's what I ask, frogs?"

"Oh, belly up in a pond
"Or down a snake's throat,
"Cuisse de Grenouille,
"Or winged death from the sky.
"And what about you, cat?"

"Dumped into an ashcan,
"Squashed flat by a car,
"Or starved amongst plenty,
"Sometimes they poison us.
"How do you beat it, frogs?"

"We spawn eggs by the hundreds,
"We lay them in lily ponds
"Where they turn into tadpoles.
"What is your system, cat?"

"We have litters of kittens,
"Eight or ten at a time,
"And boyfriends a-plenty.
"But what gives with your eggs, frogs?"

"It's just all too silly.
"The fish come and eat them,
"Eat the eggs and the tadpoles.
"And what of your kittens, cat?"

"People take them and drown them,
"Drown them in buckets,
"Our beautiful kittens.
"What can you do, frogs?"

"Lay many more eggs
"Than the fish can eat, cat."

"We hide our kittens
"So people can't find them, frogs."

"Isn't it stupid, cat, stupid and silly, cat?"

"Isn't it silly frogs, silly and stupid, frogs?"

"Why do we do it, cat?"

"Why do we do it, frogs?"

Jiggarum, juggarum, Purrrrrr-Miaow,
Two frogs on a stump,
One cat on a stump,
You tell us the meaning of life, my friends.

APPLICATION

Ahem!
I am available.
I have no home,
No friends,
And no immediate prospects.

Not to give you a hardluck story,
But things have not been going so well with me lately.
I had a nice family
But the old lady died
And the man hated cats
So out I went.

You can see I know how to look after myself,
Though I don't know for how much longer
In a filthy street
And no decent place to clean up.
I've been used to good things.

Housebroken? Of course,
Completely.
I am rather loyal.

I would be your cat—
Show it, I mean
When people come to visit,
By making a fuss over you,
And responding when you called me.

I'm not too finicky about food,
Food! Oh dear!
My stomach is empty
And my heart is desolate.

I'm not meant to be a street cat,
Or make myself a furtive shadow
In an alley.
I'm lonely, lonely, lonely,
And frightened!
Please may I come in?

Nursery Rhymes for Kittens

QUESTION

One, two, three,
Kitten up a tree.
Can he get down again?
Well, we shall see.

RUN KITTEN RUN

The dew's still on the meadow
The day has just begun
Run kitten, run kitten, run kitten run

It's time you were astir
To greet the rising sun
Run kitten, run kitten, run kitten run

The day is all too short
There's so much to be done
Run kitten, run kitten, run kitten run

The mice are in the kitchen
There are battles to be won
Run kitten, run kitten, run kitten run

The rats are in the corncrib
Hurry, kill them every one
Run kitten, run kitten, run kitten run

Oh speed thee gallant little friend
You'll be missing all the fun
Run kitten, run kitten, run, run, run, run, run.

INVITATION

House mouse, titmouse, field mouse, vole,
Mouse in the wainscoting, mouse in the hole
Town mouse, country mouse, church mouse gray
Won't you please come out to us, we only want to play,
Oh yes, all we really want is just to play.

Mouse in the kitchen closet, mouse in the bin,
Pantry mouse, parlor mouse, fat mouse and thin
Attic mouse, cellar mouse, dancing mouse so gay,
Won't you please come out to us, we only wish to play
Honestly, that's all we want, just a little play.

Oh poor mouse, bruised mouse, mouse without a head
Torn mouse, squashed mouse, mouse so very dead
Silly mouse, trusting mouse, what is there we can say
We meant no harm in asking you to come on out to play
We're really very sorry, we *only* meant to play.

MAN

Long nose
Silly clothes
No paws
Useless claws
Harsh cry
False eye
Talk, talk
Monkey walk
No fur
No purr
Face pale
No tail
Rotten planners
No manners
Big bragger
Just swagger
Lives in cell
Bad smell
Self admire
Big liar
Unjust
Can't trust
Friend untrue
M-A-N that's YOU.

WIEGENLIED

Slumber, my catkins, my get, my make
Holding you close, I'll be here when you wake
Softly sleep, softly dream, mother is nigh
Sleep tightly and dream to my purr lullaby.

THE CATNIP DANCE

Oh, the catnip dance, the catnip dance
Come and join the catnip dance
Leap in the air and then touch down
And away we go, around and around
Fly away, fly away, higher and higher
With a catnip flame and a catnip fire
Roll in the catnip
Whirl in the catnip
Jig in the catnip
Pirouette and prance
Come along, come along, come along
All cats join in the catnip dance.

RICH CAT, POOR CAT

Rich cat, poor cat
Beggar cat, tramp
House cat, alley cat
Store cat, champ.

The rich cat eats from a porcelain dish
Cream and chicken and lobster and fish
Poor cat sups from a dirty old tin
Scraps and bones and bits of skin
If you look at it, it's fair to neither
There ain't no justice in our world either.

NOT ON THE BED

Puss in the corner
Puss on the stairs
Puss in the basket
Puss on the chairs
Puss in the pantry
Puss in the shed
Puss may go everywhere
But NOT ON THE BED.

CHIMERA

I saw something, I saw something
Something moving, something jumping.
I watched it, I stalked it
I pounced on it and caught it
Oh yes, I'm sure I caught it
But when I looked it wasn't there
I couldn't find it anywhere
I know that it was there because
I had it in between my paws
Somehow it must have got away
Of course I know it's only play
I just imagined it for fun
Someday I'll catch a really one.

BATH CALL

Ickitty Pickitty Kittiky Kat
Possumy Pussomy Porsomy Rat
Mimmery Mammary Mummery Miaow
All kittens come and get washed NOW.

THE HIGH PLACE

Up high is where I like to go
Watching people down below
That's why you find me up a tree
Where no one can look down on me.

DINNER LINEUP

Pussywillow, pussywallow
All the milk that you can swallow.
Three tails up, one tail down
Hurry up and move along it's my turn now.

SURPRISE

Cat behind a curtain
Nobody can see
I peek out
I jump out
Don't you be frightened
You can be certain
It's only me.

EARLY WASHING

A kitten,
A kattern,
A dirty cat's a slattern.
A lick here
A lick there,
I can't reach my tail end
But does it really matter?